# Serve up a top grade with CGP!

Struggling with sauces?  Confused between calcium and carbs?
Fear not, this CGP revision guide is here to help...

It contains everything you need to know for the WJEC Eduqas exam,
from basic cooking methods to the "hang on, isn't this science?" parts
— plus plenty of questions to test how well you're digesting it all.

At the back, you'll find well-seasoned advice pages for the exam
and non-exam assessments, and a super-handy glossary for garnish.

# CGP — still the best!  ☺

Our sole aim here at CGP is to produce the highest quality books —
carefully written, immaculately presented and dangerously close to being funny.

Then we work our socks off to get them out to you
— at the cheapest possible prices.

# Contents

## Section Four — Where Food Comes From

## Section Five — Factors Affecting Food Choice

## Section Six — Preparation and Cooking Techniques

Published by CGP

Editors:
Liam Dyer, Rob Harrison, Simon Little, Sean Walsh.

Contributors:
Angela Nugent

With thanks to Ana Pungartnik for the copyright research.

Photo on p 4 Science Photo Library and p 24 Mark Sykes/Science Photo Library

Photo on p 2 KMI Images / Alamy Stock Photo, p 25 Food and Drink Photos / Alamy Stock Photo,
p 26 funkyfood London - Paul Williams / Alamy Stock Photo, p 30 Dale O'Dell / Alamy Stock Photo,
p 31 Westend61 GmbH / Alamy Stock Photo and Myrleen Pearson / Alamy Stock Photo.

Definition of food security on page 51: © FAO 2006 Food Security Page 1.
Available: http://www.fao.org/forestry/13128-0e6f36f27e0091055bec28ebe830f46b3.pdf [14/12/2016]

ISBN: 978 1 78294 652 6

Printed by Elanders Ltd, Newcastle upon Tyne.
Clipart from Corel®

# Proteins

Proteins, fats and carbohydrates are macronutrients. 'Macro' means large, and funnily enough our bodies need these macronutrients in large amounts. First up we have proteins — don't say we never treat you...

## Protein *is Needed for Growth, Repair* and Maintenance

1) We get protein from a wide range of foods, including: meat, fish, dairy products, nuts, seeds and beans.

2) Our bodies need proteins for a variety of reasons:

- Growth — e.g. from childhood to adulthood, and for the growth of nails, hair and muscle mass.
- Repair — e.g. repairing our muscles, tissues and organs after illness or injury.
- Maintenance — e.g. to make enzymes for digestion and antibodies to stop us getting ill.

3) Proteins are made up of amino acids — these can be thought of as the building blocks of the body.

4) Our bodies can make some amino acids (these are called non-essential amino acids). There are 11 non-essential amino acids, including: alanine, asparagine, aspartic acid and glutamic acid.

5) We have to eat the amino acids that our bodies can't make (these are called essential amino acids). There are 9 essential amino acids: histidine, isoleucine, leucine, lysine, methionine, phenylalanine, threonine, tryptophan and valine.

## Proteins *Have Different Biological Values*

- High biological value (HBV) proteins contain all of the essential amino acids we need.
- They're mainly found in animal sources — e.g. meat, fish, poultry, eggs, cheese and milk.
- Soya beans and quinoa are plant-based HBV protein foods (see next page).

- Low biological value (LBV) proteins are missing one or more of the essential amino acids we need.
- They're only found in plant sources — e.g. peas, lentils, nuts, seeds and most beans, and in smaller amounts in vegetables like spinach and broccoli.

## Protein Complementation Combines *LBV Protein Foods*

1) If we don't get enough HBV protein, we have to combine different LBV proteins to get all the essential amino acids in our diet — this is called protein complementation.

2) For example, hummus and pitta are LBV protein foods (they're missing some essential amino acids), but when we combine the two, the meal as a whole provides all the essential amino acids we need.

With compliments of the chef...

3) If you're eating a balanced diet, you probably combine proteins without realising it — e.g. a vegetable lasagne with six different veggies in the recipe is good protein complementation.

## Different People *Need Different Amounts* of Protein

1) Dietary reference values are estimates of the amount of nutrients people should have in their diet.

2) An average male should consume 55 g and an average female should consume 45 g of protein each day.

3) In reality, the amount of protein different people need varies:

- Growing children need a greater amount of protein relative to their size and body mass.
- Physically active people need more protein for muscle growth and repair.
- Pregnant women need about 6 g more protein than normal to help the baby grow. During breastfeeding, women require even more.

# Proteins

I won't pro-tend this stuff is particularly exciting, but proteins are very important to our health...

## Too Much *or* Too Little Protein Causes Problems

An excess (too much) or deficiency (too little) of protein in the diet can have serious consequences:

### Excess

- The liver and the kidneys help process proteins. Too much protein in the diet puts a lot of pressure and strain on these organs, which can be dangerous.

### Deficiency

- Without protein, growth is slowed down, especially in children who are still growing.
- Because hair, skin and nails don't grow as fast, they can get into a poor condition.
- The immune system can't work properly without protein — this means wounds don't heal as quickly and people have a higher risk of catching infections.
- People struggle to digest food properly, which means some nutrients aren't taken in by the body.
- Protein deficiency can also lead to oedema — a build up of fluid in the body that causes swelling (often around the feet).
- In severe cases, a disease called kwashiorkor can develop. A symptom of the disease is oedema around the stomach, which is why some severely malnourished children have swollen abdomens.

## There are Now Loads of Alternative Proteins

1) Vegetarians don't eat meat, so they need to get their protein from elsewhere.

2) Beans, lentils and nuts are all good sources of protein, as are eggs. There are also alternative proteins:

**Soya**
- Soya beans are one of the few plant-based HBV protein sources.
- They can be eaten whole (but must be cooked to remove toxicity) in salads, used to make soya milk and processed to make other protein alternatives like tofu and TVP...

**Mycoprotein**
- Traditionally made from a mushroom-like fungus and egg white (although there are now vegan alternatives that use potato starch instead).
- It's often used where you'd normally use chicken, and is available as chunks (e.g. for stir-fries), mince (e.g. for chilli con carne) or fillets (e.g. to serve in sauces).

**TVP**
- TVP (Textured Vegetable Protein) is also made from soya beans — specifically soya flour (made by grinding soya beans).
- The soya flour is used to make a dough which when baked has a meat-like texture and can be made into sausages, burgers and ready meals.

**Tofu**
- Tofu is made by curdling soya milk.
- It can have different textures depending on how much water it contains: it can be soft (for use in desserts and dips), firm (for use in stir-fries) and extra firm (this is sometimes called dry tofu because it has the least amount of water).

3) Alternative proteins usually don't taste of much on their own. Luckily, they're great at absorbing the flavours of the foods they're cooked in, e.g. sauces and marinades. There's also a massive range of pre-prepared flavoured alternatives, e.g. bacon-style slices, meat-free chicken fillets, etc.

## *That youth's no amateur... he's a pro-teen...*

Remember the functions of proteins using 'Really Good Macronutrient' (RGM) — repair, growth and maintenance.

Q1 Explain the difference between non-essential amino acids and essential amino acids. [2 marks]

# Fats

While it's easy to assume fats are really unhealthy, they're actually an <u>essential</u> part of our <u>daily diet</u>. And just when I was starting to feel guilty about my tower-high stack of chocolate fudge cake...

## *Fats* Provide Energy, Nutrients *and* Insulation

Our bodies need <u>fats</u> and <u>oils</u> (sometimes referred to as <u>lipids</u>) for a <u>variety of reasons</u>:

- They provide a <u>concentrated source</u> of <u>energy</u> (<u>twice as much energy</u> per gram as <u>proteins</u> and <u>carbs</u>).
- They're a source of <u>fat-soluble vitamins</u> (e.g. <u>A</u> and <u>D</u> — p.7) and help the body <u>absorb</u> these vitamins.
- They're a source of <u>essential fatty acids</u> (<u>omega-3</u> and <u>omega-6</u> fatty acids — see next page).
- Fat forms an insulating layer under our skin which helps to <u>keep us warm</u>.
- These layers of fat also protect our <u>bones</u> and organs (e.g. our <u>heart</u> and <u>kidneys</u>).
- Our bodies use fat to make <u>cholesterol</u>, a fatty substance that is an essential part of all cell membranes. However, too much cholesterol can be bad for us (see next page).

## *Fats Contain* Saturated *and* Unsaturated *Fatty Acids*

A triglyceride

1) Fats are made up of <u>fatty acids</u> and <u>glycerol</u> in the form of <u>triglycerides</u>.
2) <u>Fatty acid chains</u> are made of <u>carbon</u> and <u>hydrogen</u>. They can be <u>saturated</u> or <u>unsaturated</u> — the difference is in how <u>carbon atoms</u> bond with <u>hydrogen atoms</u>:

3) Our body breaks fat down into <u>fatty acids</u> during digestion — the ratio of saturated to unsaturated fatty acids decides whether it's a <u>saturated</u> or <u>unsaturated fat</u>.

## *Saturated Fats* are Bad for Your Health...

1) <u>Saturated fats</u> are classed as unhealthy fats, especially if eaten in large amounts.
2) They're generally <u>solid</u> at <u>room temperature</u> and tend to come from <u>animal sources</u> such as meats (including processed meats like sausages and burgers), butter, lard, suet and cheese, but they can also come from <u>plant sources</u> like <u>coconut butter</u>.
3) <u>Too much</u> saturated fat in the diet can <u>increase cholesterol levels</u> in the blood, which can increase the risk of <u>cardiovascular disease</u> (see next page).

## *... Unsaturated Fats* are Generally Healthier

1) <u>Unsaturated fats</u> are usually healthier than saturated fats.
2) They're generally soft or liquid at room temperature and come from <u>vegetable sources</u> that are high in fat (e.g. flax seeds and peanuts) and vegetable <u>oils</u> (e.g. sunflower, rapeseed and olive oils).
3) Unsaturated fats can be <u>monounsaturated</u> and <u>polyunsaturated</u>:

- <u>Monounsaturated</u> fats contain <u>one C=C double bond</u> in their carbon chains.
- They are found in foods such as <u>olive oil</u>, <u>almonds</u>, <u>peanut butter</u> and <u>avocados</u>.

- <u>Polyunsaturated</u> fats contain <u>more than one C=C double bond</u>.
- They are found in foods such as <u>sesame oil</u>, <u>soybean oil</u>, <u>seeds</u> and <u>oily fish</u>.

4) Replacing the saturated fats in your diet with unsaturated fats has been shown to <u>lower blood cholesterol</u> — this is why unsaturated fats are often referred to as 'good' fats.

# Fats

Without enough fat in our diet, our bodies wouldn't be able to function properly. However, before we get carried away and start bathing ourselves in butter, too much fat can lead to some very serious health problems...

## Omega-3 and Omega-6 Fatty Acids are Essential Fatty Acids

Our body can't produce omega-3 and omega-6 essential fatty acids, so we have to consume them as part of our diet.

- Omega-3 fatty acids are found in foods such as oily fish and seeds — they help our brain function and may reduce the risk of heart disease.
- Omega-6 fatty acids are found in foods such as chicken, nuts and vegetable oils — they help to lower blood cholesterol and reduce inflammation.

Some people take fish-oil capsules to get their dose of omega-3 fatty acids.

## Fats Should Make Up Less Than 35% of Our Daily Food Energy

- According to government guidelines, fat should make up no more than 35% of our food energy per day (see p.16), with no more than 11% coming from saturated fat.
- It's recommended that an average adult consume 70 g of fat every day, with a maximum of 20 g of this being saturated fat.

As with protein, the amount of fat a person needs may change depending on age and physical activity.

## We Need the Right Amount of Fat in Our Diet

A fat excess (too much fat) or fat deficiency (too little fat) can be unhealthy and dangerous:

### Excess

- Too much fat can lead to weight gain, where excess fat is stored under the skin (and around organs in some cases).
- Excessive levels of fat in the body can lead to obesity (see p.14). Obesity can lead to diet-related health issues like type-2 diabetes (see p.15), where the body struggles to control blood sugar levels.
- Too much saturated fat in the diet can increase blood cholesterol levels, restricting blood flow and increasing the risk of high blood pressure and cardiovascular disease, e.g. CHD, a stroke or heart attack (see p.14).

Excess fat in the diet can lead to the build-up of fat around vital organs like the heart (yellow fat can be seen around the red heart muscle).

### Deficiency

- A lack of fat in the diet means that less fat-soluble vitamins (including A and D) are absorbed by the body. This causes vitamin deficiency, which leads to various health issues (see p.7).
- If there's also a lack of carbohydrate in the diet, the body will start to use its fat store for energy. Therefore, not eating enough fat can lead to weight loss if there's also a lack of carbohydrate in the diet.
- Less body fat means there's less insulation to keep the body warm, and so a person with a fat deficiency may become colder faster.
- It also means there will be a thinner layer of fat under the skin to protect the body from knocks.

## Give up my weekly barn dancing class? Fat chance!

It's important you know the differences between saturated and unsaturated fats. A really simple way to get them stuck in your head is to draw out a quick table of all the differences — it's guaranteed to get any party started...

Q1 Give two foods that are high in saturated fat. [2 marks]

Q2 Describe two problems that are associated with a fat deficiency in the diet. [2 marks]

# Carbohydrates

Carbohydrates are the final macronutrient we have to look at, whoopee.  Get your teeth into this stuff...

## *Carbohydrates are Needed for Energy*

Carbohydrates can be split into two main types: sugar and starch:

- Sugar, e.g. glucose and fructose, can be found in food naturally (e.g. sugars in fruits and vegetables), or can be added to food during the manufacturing process (e.g. sugars in cakes, sweets and fizzy pop).
- Added sugars are often referred to as 'empty calories' because they have no nutritional benefit other than energy.

- Starch can be found in foods such as potatoes, bread, pasta, rice and cereals, as well as vegetables and fruit (in smaller amounts).
- Starchy foods contain lots of nutrients including B vitamins, iron and calcium.
- Wholegrain starch foods also have really high fibre content (see p.10).

When we eat carbohydrate-based foods, our body breaks down the sugar and starch into glucose, which is absorbed into our blood and used by our body for energy.

## *Simple Carbohydrates are Digested Quickly...*

Simple carbohydrates such as sugar can be divided into monosaccharides and disaccharides:

Monosaccharides are the most basic sugar molecules, e.g. glucose and fructose.

glucose  fructose

Disaccharides are made up of two monosaccharides, e.g. sucrose is made up of glucose and fructose.

sucrose

'Sugary' foods like cakes, jams and sweets are mainly made up of simple carbohydrates.

The body rapidly digests simple carbohydrates, making blood sugar levels rise quickly and providing a short burst of energy.

## *...While Complex Ones Take Longer to Digest*

Complex carbohydrates include 'starchy' foods like wholewheat bread and potatoes.

Complex carbohydrates such as starch are polysaccharides:

Polysaccharides are made up of lots of monosaccharides joined together, e.g. starches are made up of lots of glucose molecules.

... starch

Complex carbohydrates take a lot longer to digest than simple ones, so they gradually increase blood sugar levels and provide a slow, steady release of energy.

## *The Glycaemic Index Shows How Carbs Affect Blood Sugar Levels*

The glycaemic index (GI) rates carbohydrates on how quickly they affect blood sugar levels:

- High GI foods are digested quickly and cause a rapid rise in blood sugar levels — high GI foods include white bread/pasta/rice, cornflakes and watermelon.
- Low GI foods are digested slowly and cause a gradual rise in blood sugar levels — low GI foods include wholewheat bread/pasta, brown rice, peaches and porridge.

The glycaemic index is especially helpful to people with diabetes because it allows them to choose low GI carbohydrates so they can avoid surges in blood sugar levels.

Section One — Food, Nutrition and Health

# Carbohydrates

I don't know about you, but I'm in the mood for another page all about carbohydrates — no, just me?...

## 50% of Our Energy Should Come from Carbs

According to government guidelines, carbohydrates should make up approximately half of our food energy per day (see p.16).

- Ideally, most of this energy should come from starchy foods and natural sugars such as those found in bread, pasta, fruit and veg.
- Free sugars, such as those added to food and drinks during manufacturing and those found in sweet foods like syrups and fruit juice, should make up no more than 5%.

Unfortunately, cucumber face masks don't count towards daily food energy.

On average, people in the UK consume too much sugar. To help with this, food labelling not only has a section for total carbohydrates, but it also has an extra section called 'of which sugars' — this helps people separate their sugar intake from their total carb intake (see p.65).

## Eating Too Much or Too Little Carbohydrate is Unhealthy

Like with fat and protein, too much (excess) or too little (deficiency) carbohydrate in our diet is unhealthy and can have serious effects on how our body functions:

### Excess

- If we take in more energy from carbohydrates than our body uses, the extra carbohydrate is converted into fat. Too much fat causes obesity and other diet-related health issues (see p.14-15).
- Sugars are the worst for this because they're digested quickly, meaning the energy they provide is ready to use almost immediately — if it's not used quickly, we store it as fat.
- Eating too much sugary food can lead to dental caries (see p.15). Free sugars are the worst type of sugar for dental caries — e.g. mango juice is more likely to cause dental caries than if you ate chunks of mango because the sugars are already released and ready to attack your teeth.
- Because simple carbohydrates (e.g. sugar) are quickly digested, they cause rapid surges in blood sugar levels (see previous page). If our blood sugar levels fluctuate (move up and down) too wildly it can lead to the development of type 2 diabetes (see p.15).

The natural sugars in whole fruits are much better for our teeth than the free sugars found in fruit juices.

### Deficiency

- A lack of carbohydrate in our diet causes our blood sugar level to drop. This drop can cause hunger, dizziness and tiredness because our body has less energy than it needs.
- If our bodies don't have enough carbohydrate for energy, they need to find another source of energy and will start to use up fat in the diet or body.
- If we also have a fat deficiency then our bodies start to use up protein — this causes us to lose muscle, which makes us weaker.

## My parrot loves starch — she's called Polly Saccharide...

That's it for macronutrients. As the name suggests, they're a large part of our nutrition and you need to know the role each of them plays in our diet. They'll show up again later, so it's best to learn them now.

Q1    Name the type of carbohydrate that releases its energy slowly.    [1 mark]

Q2    Name one diet-related health problem associated with too much carbohydrate in the diet.    [1 mark]

# Vitamins — Fat-Soluble

Vitamins, minerals and trace elements are all micronutrients — we need them in small amounts. Vitamins are organic compounds (they come from plants and animals) and are used in processes that keep us alive and well.

## Vitamins A and D are Fat-Soluble

1) Fat-soluble vitamins are found in fatty foods (e.g. meat, fish, animal-based products and vegetable oils).
2) There are two fat-soluble vitamins you need to know about — meet vitamins A and D:

*There are four fat-soluble vitamins, but you don't need to know about the other two (vitamins E and K).*

### Vitamin A Helps Us to See in the Dark

- Vitamin A is needed for good eyesight (especially night vision), growth, a healthy immune system and skin.
- The main source is retinol, which is found in liver, butter, oily fish and eggs, but it can also be made from carotene (found in margarine and orange or yellow fruit and veg).

**Excess**

Too much vitamin A over a period of time can weaken bones. During pregnancy, foods containing very high levels (e.g. liver) should be avoided to prevent harm to the unborn baby.

**Deficiency**

Too little vitamin A can lead to night blindness, a weaker immune system and stunted growth.

*The NHS recommends 0.7 mg of vitamin A for men and 0.6 mg for women each day.*

### Vitamin D Helps Us Absorb Calcium

- Vitamin D helps the body absorb various minerals, including calcium, which is important for the development of healthy bones and teeth.
- It's found in oily fish and egg yolks and is also produced when skin is exposed to sunlight.

**Excess**

Too much vitamin D makes you absorb too much calcium — this can lead to kidney damage.

**Deficiency**

Too little vitamin D can lead to bone diseases like osteomalacia (where bones become soft), rickets and osteoporosis (where bones become brittle, see p.15).

*The NHS recommends 0.01 mg of vitamin D a day, although in summer most of us should be able to get enough through natural exposure to the sun.*

- Any fat-soluble vitamins that aren't used up by the body are stored in fat tissue for future use. This means that we don't necessarily need to take in the same amount of each vitamin every day.
- However, we need to be careful that we don't build up an excess of these vitamins. This is unlikely to occur through a balanced diet — the main risk comes through multivitamin supplements (see p.57).

## I'm afraid this isn't a licence to eat cake every day...

Way before we knew about vitamins, the ancient Egyptians would use liver as a treatment for night blindness. These days we know why this remedy was so successful — because of the high level of fat-soluble vitamin A.

Q1    Describe the role vitamin D plays in the body.                    [1 mark]

8

# Vitamins — Water-Soluble

Water-soluble vitamins generally aren't stored in the body like fat-soluble ones, so we should take them in daily.

## B Vitamins and Vitamin C are Water-Soluble

'Water-soluble' vitamins dissolve in water — there are lots of them, but you need to know these for the exam:

| Vitamin | Function | Sources include | Problems caused by having too little |
|---|---|---|---|
| B1 Thiamin | Helps the nervous system and with energy release from foods. | Bread, pasta, rice, peas, eggs and liver. | Tiredness, weak muscles and beriberi (in severe cases) — a disease that affects the heart, blood vessels and nervous system. |
| B2 Riboflavin | Helps with energy release from foods and repair of tissues. | Milk, eggs, cheese, and leafy greens. | Dry skin, a sore throat and sores around the mouth. |
| B3 Niacin | Helps with energy release from foods and maintaining a healthy nervous system and skin. | Wheat, nuts, meat and fish. | Pellagra (a disease causing fatigue, depression and loss of memory). |
| B9 Folic Acid (or folate) | Crucial for growth and healthy babies, and works with vitamin B12 to make red blood cells. | Liver, peas and leafy greens | Anaemia, tiredness, weak muscles and mouth sores. Folic acid is especially important for women planning pregnancy as low levels at conception can cause spina bifida in babies (see p.13). |
| B12 Cobalamin | Helps the nervous system and works with vitamin B9 to make red blood cells. | Milk, eggs, meat and fish. | Tiredness and nerve damage in extreme cases. Vegans (who don't eat any animal produce) are most likely to have too little. |
| C Ascorbic acid | Protects the body from infection and allergies, keeps blood vessels healthy and heals wounds. It also helps the body absorb iron. | Citrus fruits, tomatoes, strawberries, green veg and potatoes. | Anaemia (see p.14) and scurvy (tiredness and bleeding gums). Vitamin C is an antioxidant, so too little might increase the risk of cancer. |

Water-soluble vitamins are lost in urine, so in most cases it's unlikely they'll build up to levels where there are serious side effects. However, excessive amounts of vitamin C can cause stomach pain and diarrhoea.

Arr, I've got a scurvy cutlass.

## Prepare Fruit and Veg Carefully to Keep Vitamins

1) Once exposed to air, fruits and veg start losing vitamin C, so prepare them just before you need them.
2) Don't leave your fruits and veg to stand in water because B vitamins and vitamin C dissolve into the water. Steaming or microwaving are the best ways to keep these water-soluble vitamins.
3) Don't chop fruit and veg into small pieces as it exposes more of the surface to air and water.
4) There are more nutrients in or just below the skin, so peel them thinly or use them unpeeled if possible.

## Vitamin B Group? — my dad's got one of their records...

There are lots of vitamins to remember on these pages — and yes, you need to know what they do, where they're found and the effects of getting too little (or too much). It might be helpful to write up a Post-it for each vitamin.

Q1 Give one type of food you would recommend to a person suffering from scurvy. [1 mark]

Section One — Food, Nutrition and Health

# Minerals and Trace Elements

We also need small amounts of minerals and trace elements in our diet — this nutrition lark is full of surprises...

## Calcium, Iron, Potassium and Magnesium are Minerals

Minerals are chemical elements that our bodies need in small amounts. They help in various chemical reactions in our body and are needed for a variety of reasons:

**Calcium**
- Calcium is needed for strong bones and teeth, healthy nerves and muscles and blood clotting — growing children need calcium every day to help build strong bones and teeth (see p.12).
- It's found in milk, cheese, tofu, bread, green leafy vegetables, hard water and sesame seeds.
- + Too much calcium is rare, but any excess is stored in organs like the kidneys — this can increase the risk of kidney stones and could even stop the kidneys working.
- - Too little calcium during childhood can lead to problems such as rickets and osteoporosis (see p.15) because bones become weaker. It can also slow down blood clotting.

**Iron**
- Iron is needed to form part of the haemoglobin which gives blood cells their red colour.
- It's found in dark green vegetables (e.g. spinach) and meat (especially liver and kidney).
- + Too much iron is toxic (poisonous) and can cause stomach pains, nausea and constipation. In extreme cases it can even cause death.
- - Too little iron causes a deficiency disease called anaemia (see p.14).

**Potassium**
- Potassium is needed for good cardiovascular health and for controlling the balance of fluids in our body — it even works with sodium (salt) to control our muscles and nerves.
- It's found in loads of food, including fruit and veg (especially bananas), pulses, nuts and seeds.
- + Too much potassium can cause nausea, stomach pain, weak muscles and an irregular heartbeat.
- - Too little potassium can cause an irregular heartbeat, and paralysis or heart failure in severe cases.

**Magnesium**
- Magnesium is needed to help release energy from our food and for healthy bones.
- It's found in green leafy vegetables (e.g. spinach), nuts, seeds and dark chocolate — yum.
- + Too much magnesium can cause nausea and diarrhoea.
- - Too little magnesium is rare, but it can cause nausea, lack of appetite and weak muscles.

## Fluoride and Iodine are Trace Elements

Trace elements are minerals, but we need them in even smaller amounts:

**Fluoride**
- Fluoride strengthens teeth, hardens tooth enamel and helps prevent dental caries (see p.15). The NHS recommends brushing your teeth twice a day with fluoride toothpaste.
- It's found in fish, tea, fluoridated water and dental products (toothpaste and mouthwash).
- + Too much fluoride is toxic and can lead to brown-coloured teeth, bone problems and cancer.
- - Too little fluoride can lead to weak teeth and enamel, which leads to dental caries.

**Iodine**
- Iodine is needed to make some hormones used by the body.
- It's found in seafood, dairy foods and vegetables.
- - A serious lack of iodine can cause goitre (neck swelling) and complications in unborn babies.

In addition to food, minerals and trace elements can be taken in through multivitamin supplements (p.57).

## If there's one thing all divers hate, it's hard water...

Remember, we only need a 'trace' of trace elements — because this is such a small amount they're micronutrients.

Q1 Explain the importance of fluoride in our toothpaste. [2 marks]

# Fibre and Water

As well as proteins, carbs, fats, vitamins, minerals and trace elements we also need <u>fibre</u> and <u>water</u> — blimey!

## *Fibre Isn't Digested by the Body*

1) <u>Fibre</u>, sometimes called <u>NSP</u> (non-starch polysaccharide) or '<u>roughage</u>', is a type of <u>carbohydrate</u> that helps to keep your digestive system <u>working properly</u> and keeps food <u>moving</u> through it. Fibre is found in things like:

Fibre also makes us feel fuller for longer.

- <u>Vegetables</u> — e.g. peas, beans, broccoli, carrots and potatoes (especially the skin).
- <u>Fruit</u> and <u>fruit juice</u> — raspberries, prunes, bananas, apples.
- <u>Brown bread</u> and <u>wholemeal</u> or <u>whole grain</u> foods — e.g. wholemeal bread/rice/pasta/flour.
- <u>Lentils</u>, <u>beans</u>, <u>seeds</u> and <u>nuts</u>.

2) You need to eat lots of fibre to stay <u>healthy</u>. If you don't, it can lead to <u>health problems</u> such as: <u>constipation</u>, <u>bowel</u> and <u>colon cancer</u>, <u>heart disease</u>, <u>high blood pressure</u>.

3) The NHS states that the average adult should take in <u>30 g</u> of fibre every day. <u>Young children</u> need <u>less fibre</u> because the 'fullness' fibre gives people can stop them from eating foods that contain other important nutrients.

Most people in the UK don't eat enough fibre — some of the health problems mentioned are very common in people over 40.

## *You Can't Live Without Water*

1) Around <u>60%</u> of your body is <u>water</u> — it's found in every cell of your body, as well as fluids like blood, sweat and saliva.

2) Our bodies need water to:
- <u>Eliminate waste</u> from the body (e.g. excretion)
- <u>Control body temperature</u> (e.g. sweating)
- Aid the process of <u>digestion</u>

Steve could always be found loitering by the local watering hole.

3) You get water from <u>drinks</u> like water (obviously), fruit juice, tea, lemonade, etc. It's also found in <u>food</u> — vegetables and fruit contain quite a lot, and even things like meat and bread contain water.

4) Our body loses water in a variety of ways including our sweat, breath, urine and faeces. If you don't drink enough to replace the water you've used or lost, you become <u>dehydrated</u> and your body can't <u>work properly</u>. Dehydration also causes:

- <u>Slower reactions</u> and <u>poor decision-making</u>, as your <u>brain</u> needs water to function well.
- <u>Blood to thicken</u>, making it <u>harder</u> for the <u>heart</u> to pump the blood around the body.
- An <u>increase</u> in <u>body temperature</u> (the body can't sweat effectively).

5) You should have about <u>2 litres</u> of water a day — but if you're <u>hot</u> or <u>exercising</u> you need to drink <u>more</u> to get enough water into your system.

6) <u>Overhydration</u> can also be very <u>serious</u>. It's caused by drinking <u>huge amounts</u> of water in a <u>short period of time</u>, leading to headaches, nausea and confusion. It also <u>dilutes</u> the concentration of <u>nutrients</u> in our blood — this can affect the function of organs like the <u>kidneys</u>, which in some cases can be fatal.

---

## *Fibre Optics — a range of light snacks to aid digestion...*

Don't get confused — while fibre isn't digested by the body, it plays a very important role in our digestive system.

Q1   State two ways in which water can be lost from the body.                    [2 marks]

# Healthy Eating Guidelines

The <u>government</u> issues <u>guidelines</u> on healthy eating.  Crunch some lettuce while you read all about it.

## *The Eatwell Guide Gives Recommendations for a Healthy Diet*

The <u>Eatwell Guide</u> is an easy way of showing <u>how much</u> or little of each <u>food group</u> is recommended.

<u>Fruit and vegetables:</u>
- About <u>1/3</u> of your daily food intake.
- Aim to eat at least <u>5 portions</u> of <u>fruit and veg</u> every day.

*Total calories per day*
Women: 2000 kcal
Men: 2500 kcal

<u>One portion</u> is:

<u>One piece</u> of <u>medium-sized</u> fruit, e.g. apple, banana or orange.

<u>One heaped</u> <u>tablespoon</u> of <u>dried fruit</u>, e.g. raisins, sultanas.

<u>Three heaped</u> <u>tablespoons</u> of <u>cooked vegetables</u>, e.g. carrots, sweetcorn.

150 ml of <u>fruit juices</u> or <u>smoothies</u> (only <u>one glass</u> per day).

<u>Starchy carbohydrates:</u>
- About <u>1/3</u> of your daily food intake*.
- Choose <u>higher fibre</u>, <u>wholegrain</u> options with less <u>fat</u>, <u>sugar</u> and <u>salt</u>.
- Try to include a <u>starchy</u> food in <u>every meal</u>, e.g. <u>potatoes</u>, and <u>wholegrain</u> <u>bread</u>, <u>pasta</u> and <u>cereals</u>.

*Careful here — we're talking about the <u>amount of carbs</u> you eat, not how much <u>energy</u> you get from them (p.16).

<u>Oils and spreads:</u>
- Use <u>unsaturated</u> <u>oils</u> and <u>spreads</u>, and not very often. E.g. <u>sunflower</u> and <u>olive</u> oil.

<u>Beans, pulses, fish, meat and other protein:</u>
- Aim to eat <u>two portions</u> of <u>fish</u> a week (one <u>oily</u>, e.g. <u>salmon</u>, <u>sardines</u>).
- <u>Pulses</u> are a <u>good alternative</u> to meat.
- Choose <u>lean cuts</u> of meat and eat less <u>processed meat</u> (e.g. <u>bacon</u>, <u>sausages</u>).

<u>Dairy products and alternatives:</u>
- Have <u>some dairy</u> and try <u>lower fat</u> options, e.g. <u>1% fat milk</u>, or <u>reduced-fat cheese</u>.
- You can also try dairy alternatives, such as <u>soya</u> or <u>rice-based milks</u>.

 Drink <u>6-8 glasses</u> of <u>fluids</u> a day — hydration is part of a healthy diet.

 Eat less <u>sugary</u>, <u>salty</u> and <u>fatty</u> foods, e.g. <u>muffins</u>, <u>cakes</u>, <u>biscuits</u>.

## *Food Labels Show Guidelines for an Average Adult*

<u>Reference Intakes</u> (RIs) are <u>guidelines</u> that are often shown on food <u>labels</u>.

1) RIs are based on an <u>average adult</u>, so they are only an <u>indication</u> of the amount of <u>energy</u> and <u>nutrients</u> an adult requires each day.

2) Adults will have <u>different requirements</u> depending on their <u>age</u>, <u>gender</u>, how <u>active</u> they are, and if they have any diet-related <u>health conditions</u>.

3) Food labels also list each <u>nutrient</u> in the food as a <u>percentage</u> of the RI (this can be for <u>100 g</u> of the food, per <u>portion</u>, or <u>both</u>).
   E.g. If 100 g of cake contains 9 g of sugar, it would be labelled as 10% of your RI for sugars.

| Energy / Nutrient | Reference Intake (RI) |
|---|---|
| Energy | 2000 kcal |
| Fat | 70 g |
| Saturates | 20 g |
| Carbohydrate | 260 g |
| Sugars | 90 g |
| Protein | 50 g |
| Salt | 6 g |

## *If only custard creams were 1 of your 5 a day...*

This stuff is really important — try covering up the Eatwell Guide and see if you can sketch your own from memory.

Q1  Peter has a list of the food that he ate for breakfast, lunch and dinner.

**Breakfast**: Wholemeal toast & jam
**Lunch**: Egg & cheese sandwich, crisps, chocolate, yoghurt
**Dinner**: Chicken curry & rice, cream cake.

Describe to what extent Peter meets the guidelines set out in the Eatwell Guide.        [3 marks]

# Nutritional Needs of Different Age Groups

Everyone should roughly aim to follow the healthy eating guidelines, but our nutritional needs change throughout each stage of our lives. These pages will give you the low-down.

## *Children Grow Quickly and Need Lots of Energy*

### Toddlers

1) The Eatwell Guide doesn't apply to children under two, but toddlers and children up until the age of five should gradually move towards a diet based on the Eatwell Guide.

2) Toddlers do not have large stomachs, so they should have small and frequent meals to get the energy they need.

3) Milk is an important source of nutrients — 300 ml each day gives toddlers the daily calcium they need and it's also a good source of vitamin A.

...although it's better to get calcium from a range of foods.

4) Toddlers should be frequently encouraged to try a variety of foods. Kids can be dead fussy though, so experiment mixing new foods with things they like and offer them different choices.

### Children

1) Children grow quickly and are very active, so there is an extra demand for energy and nutrients — they need more than adults (in proportion to their body size).

2) Good amounts of these nutrients are important for children:

| Nutrient | Reason | Example Foods |
|---|---|---|
| Protein | To help them grow and repair the body. | Fish fingers, boiled eggs |
| Carbohydrate | Starchy carbohydrates and some fats provide energy for growth and physical activity. Saturated fats should be eaten in moderation. | Mashed potato, pasta |
| Fat | | Peanuts, avocados |
| Calcium | For healthy teeth and bone development. | Milk, yoghurt tubes, cheese |
| Vitamin D | | Tuna, salmon |

3) Foods high in sugar should be eaten infrequently, and only ever at mealtimes. Too many of these foods can cause tooth decay and weight gain.

4) Eating habits of children may be adopted from their parents, so families should eat healthily together.

### Teenagers

1) Teenagers should aim for a balanced diet, according to the Eatwell Guide.

2) Rapid growth spurts happen around the early teens — girls usually start these earlier than boys.

3) Good amounts of these nutrients are important for teenagers:

| Nutrient | Reason | Example Foods |
|---|---|---|
| Protein | To cope with growth spurts. Boys tend to need more protein than girls as muscular tissue develops. | Omelettes, chicken |
| Iron | Teenage girls lose iron when they have their period so it needs to be replaced or they could become anaemic (p.14). Vitamin C helps the body absorb the iron. | Spinach, beef |
| Vitamin C | | Peppers, strawberries |
| Calcium | The skeleton grows quickly during this time. These nutrients are necessary as they help the skeleton reach peak size and bone density. | Milk, yoghurt, kale, tofu |
| Vitamin D | | Tuna, salmon, mackerel |

4) During the teen years there can be lots of stress (e.g. exams, media pressure) which affect eating habits — stress can lead to conditions like anorexia, but also overeating which can cause obesity.

# Nutritional Needs of Different Age Groups

Here are some more life stages that you have to look forward to. You may as well start planning now...

## Adults Stop Growing and Nutritional Needs Don't Vary Much

### Early / Middle Adulthood

1) Growth and development stops, so adults should focus on maintaining a healthy lifestyle — they are encouraged to follow the Eatwell Guide to keep the body disease-free.

2) Men usually require more calories than women because they have more lean muscle (muscles require lots of energy to function properly) and are generally taller and larger.

3) Iron is especially important for adult women as they continue to lose it through periods.

4) Calcium and vitamin D are important for all adults to reduce the chance of bone diseases in later life — women can quickly lose bone strength after the menopause in their 40s or 50s too, so these nutrients are needed to keep the skeleton strong.

5) During pregnancy, women should adapt their diet to help the baby. Pregnant women should:

- eat about 200 more calories per day towards the end of the pregnancy to support the baby's growth. They should be careful not to overeat as it can cause excessive weight gain.
- consume more folic acid — it helps to reduce the risk of birth defects such as spina bifida.

### Late Adulthood

1) As we age, our muscle mass decreases and it can become more difficult to do physical exercise - elderly adults can gain body fat if their diet doesn't change.

2) Elderly adults need to take great care with their energy intake — cutting down on excess saturated fats will help avoid health risks like coronary heart disease (see next page).

3) The senses of taste and smell change, which can affect the enjoyment of food. Recipes and meals need to be adapted to make them appealing and interesting.

4) Elderly adults have similar nutritional requirements to younger adults, but they must make sure they get enough:

| Nutrient | Reason | Example Foods |
|---|---|---|
| Calcium | To help stop bones becoming weak and brittle and reduce the risk of developing bone diseases. | Milk, yoghurt, kale, sardines |
| Vitamin D | | Tuna, salmon, mackerel |
| Vitamin B12 | To keep the brain healthy and prevent memory loss. | Milk, fish, beef |
| Fibre | To help prevent constipation as the digestive system begins to weaken. | Lentils, wholemeal bread |
| Vitamin A | To help maintain good eyesight. | Liver, scrambled eggs |

5) Vitamin supplements are useful if your diet doesn't contain enough, e.g. less active elderly adults may not get enough vitamin D from sunlight, so may benefit from vitamin D tablets.

## Oh, I thought supplements helped you be more flexible...

In the exam you might be asked to plan a meal for a certain age group — although nutrients are important throughout our lives, you need to pinpoint why your meal would benefit that age group in particular.

Q1 Explain the importance of each nutrient for the groups listed below:

a) Calcium for toddlers [1 mark]

b) Protein for teenagers [1 mark]

c) Folic acid for pregnant women [1 mark]

d) Vitamin B12 for elderly adults [1 mark]

# Diet-Related Health Problems

A <u>bad diet</u> will affect your <u>health</u>, and certain <u>diseases</u> affect your <u>nutritional needs</u>.

## *Obesity is When the Body Has Too Much Fat*

1) Obesity is <u>very common</u> — it affects roughly <u>one</u> in every <u>four</u> adults in the UK.

2) <u>Body Mass Index</u> (BMI) is often used to check if someone is overweight or obese.

3) For adults, a BMI between <u>18.5</u> and <u>25</u> is classed as a <u>healthy weight</u>, between <u>25</u> and <u>30</u> as <u>overweight</u>, between <u>30</u> and <u>35</u> as <u>obese</u> and above <u>35</u> as <u>extremely obese</u>.

> *Working out BMI*
> Divide your weight (kg)
> by your height (m)
> and divide the answer by
> your height again.

BMI is not always a reliable indicator of someone's body fat — a person could weigh a lot (and have a high BMI) due to a large amount of muscle mass rather than body fat.

| Causes | Health Problems |
|---|---|
| • An <u>incorrect balance of energy</u> — a person consumes <u>more calories</u> than they <u>burn off</u>.<br>• Eating lots of <u>food</u> high in <u>fat</u> and <u>sugar</u>.<br>• Having a <u>sedentary lifestyle</u>. | • <u>High blood pressure</u> and <u>high cholesterol</u> increase the chance of <u>cardiovascular disease</u> (see below).<br>• There's a <u>greater risk</u> of other <u>serious</u> health conditions such as <u>type 2 diabetes</u>, <u>liver disease</u> and <u>cancer</u>.<br>• <u>Breathing difficulties</u>, <u>tiredness</u> and <u>low self-esteem</u> are also common. |

A sedentary lifestyle is one with little or no physical activity.

## *Cardiovascular Disease is Often Caused by Clogged Arteries*

1) <u>Cardiovascular disease</u> (CVD) refers to any disease related to the <u>heart</u> or <u>blood vessels</u>.

2) The most common type is <u>coronary heart disease</u> (CHD) — <u>arteries</u> (which <u>supply</u> the heart with blood full of <u>oxygen</u>) are <u>narrowed</u>, because they are <u>filled</u> with <u>fatty deposits</u>.

3) CHD can lead to <u>angina</u>, <u>heart attacks</u> and <u>strokes</u>:

| Causes | Health Problems |
|---|---|
| • Eating lots of <u>saturated fats</u>.<br>• Being <u>physically inactive</u> — because <u>exercise</u> keeps the heart and the <u>cardiovascular system</u> healthy.<br>• <u>Smoking</u> — damages the lining of <u>arteries</u> and reduces the oxygen in the blood.<br>• High <u>blood pressure</u>. | • Blood cannot pass through your blood vessels <u>efficiently</u>, which can cause a <u>squeezing pain</u> in your chest (<u>angina</u>).<br>• <u>Blood clots</u> can form and block <u>blood flow</u>.<br>• <u>Strokes</u> occur when blood flow to the <u>brain</u> is blocked, and <u>heart attacks</u> occur when blood flow to the <u>heart</u> is blocked (both can be <u>fatal</u>). |

<u>Blood pressure</u> is how much pressure the blood puts against the walls of your <u>arteries</u>.
High blood pressure puts <u>strain</u> on <u>blood vessels</u> and <u>organs</u> and can increase the risk of <u>CHD</u> / <u>strokes</u>.

## *Anaemia can be Caused by Iron Deficiency*

1) <u>Iron</u> is needed to make <u>red blood cells</u> — these cells carry <u>oxygen</u> from the lungs and travel in your blood around the body to where it is needed.

2) People with <u>anaemia</u> have a <u>reduced amount</u> of <u>red blood cells</u>.

| Causes | Health Problems |
|---|---|
| • Not eating enough <u>iron-rich foods</u>, e.g. <u>red meat</u> and <u>dark green leafy vegetables</u>.<br>• Women lose iron during their <u>periods</u>.<br>• <u>Pregnant women</u> lose iron to their baby during pregnancy. | • <u>tiredness</u><br>• <u>pale complexion</u><br>• <u>heart palpitations</u><br>• <u>headaches</u><br>• abnormal <u>fingernails</u> |

Warning: iron deficiency.

# Diet-Related Health Problems

Oh, there's another page on this? Sorry, you just can't get away with having a <u>poor diet</u> scot-free.

## *Diabetes Lets Your Blood Glucose Levels Run Out of Control*

1) <u>Insulin</u> is a <u>hormone</u> that allows <u>glucose</u> to be <u>absorbed</u> by cells in the body.

2) Insulin is created in the <u>pancreas</u> — if there is <u>too much glucose</u> in the blood, the pancreas <u>produces</u> insulin to <u>reduce</u> the <u>blood glucose level</u>.

3) <u>Type 2 diabetes</u> is a disorder where blood glucose levels stay too high because the pancreas either can't <u>produce enough insulin</u> or the <u>body resists it</u>.

*There are two types of diabetes — <u>type 1</u> and <u>type 2</u>. You'll only need to learn about type 2.*

**Causes**
- Being <u>overweight</u> or <u>obese</u>.
- <u>Excessive sugar</u> in the diet can lead to obesity (increasing the risk of type 2 diabetes) — this is affecting more <u>young people</u>.

**Health Problems**
- Diabetes can cause <u>long-term health problems</u> such as <u>poor eyesight</u> (or even <u>blindness</u>), <u>limb numbness</u>, <u>kidney failure</u> and <u>cardiovascular diseases</u> such as CHD.
- People with diabetes can feel <u>tired</u> and <u>thirsty</u>.
- The body <u>flushes</u> out <u>glucose</u> by <u>passing urine</u> more often.

## *Poor Diet Can Affect the Skeleton Too*

Your <u>bones</u> and <u>teeth</u> can become <u>diseased</u> if you don't get the <u>right amount</u> of nutrients.

**Rickets**
- <u>Rickets</u> is a condition that means that the <u>bones</u> are <u>soft</u> and <u>weak</u>.
- This occurs in <u>children</u> if they don't have enough <u>vitamin D</u> or <u>calcium</u> — e.g. little exposure to <u>sunlight</u> or not eating enough <u>foods</u> rich in these nutrients.
- Rickets causes <u>pain</u> in the bones, increases the chances of <u>fracturing bones</u> and can cause physical <u>deformities</u>, e.g. <u>bowed legs</u>.

*Both of these are linked to a lack of vitamin D or calcium — think of some example foods for different age groups that would help prevent these conditions.*

**Osteoporosis**
- Osteoporosis is a <u>bone disease</u> which <u>weakens</u> bones and makes them <u>brittle</u>, increasing the chance of breaking bones from <u>simple falls</u> (called fragility fractures).
- It is <u>common</u> in older people because <u>bone density</u> is lost <u>naturally</u> as we age.
- Women tend to lose bone density <u>more rapidly</u> after the <u>menopause</u>.
- Eating foods rich in <u>vitamin D</u> or <u>calcium</u> can help prevent osteoporosis.

**Dental Caries**
- <u>Plaque</u> is a <u>sticky substance</u> that contains lots of <u>bacteria</u> — it <u>builds up</u> on your teeth over time from <u>leftover food</u>.
- Bacteria <u>feed</u> on <u>sugars</u> and create <u>acids</u> that can <u>destroy tooth enamel</u> and cause <u>dental caries</u> (also called <u>tooth decay</u>).
- <u>Brushing</u> your <u>teeth</u> with <u>fluoride toothpaste</u> twice a day and eating <u>fewer</u> foods <u>high in sugar</u> can help <u>prevent</u> dental caries.

## *My cardiovascular system never loved me — such heartache...*

Make sure you learn how to prevent diabetes and skeletal problems before covering the pages and scribbling down as much information as possible. Rinse and repeat until you're fluent in diet-related diseases.

Q1 Explain two ways that someone could prevent / reduce the risk of developing:

a) obesity [2 marks]  b) cardiovascular disease [2 marks]

# Energy Needs

You know what we need more of? Acronyms, that's right. BMR, PAL and LOL are all key terms to do with energy and the diet that you'll need to know (alright, I lied about one of them).

## BMR is the Minimum Energy Needed to Function

1) Basal Metabolic Rate (BMR) is the smallest amount of energy needed for you to stay alive — this is stuff you don't think about, like breathing and keeping your heart beating.

2) These basic life processes can use up to about 75% of the energy we use each day — other things like digestion and physical activity make up the rest.

3) There are many factors that affect a person's BMR.

> The average BMR for an adult is about 1500 — 2000 calories.

- Age — BMR decreases as we get older due to reduction of muscle mass.
- Gender — Women, in general, have a lower BMR than men as they're generally smaller and tend to have less muscle.
- Weight and height — Heavier or larger bodies need more calories, so have a higher BMR.
- Exercise — Again, it's all about the muscle — regular exercise (especially strength training) increases muscle, which raises your BMR.

## PAL is a Way to Express Your Physical Activity

Competitive gymnast
PAL = about 2.0

1) Your Physical Activity Level (PAL) is a measure of how active you are/how much exercise you get.

2) If you are more active, e.g. a competitive gymnast, you will have a higher PAL than someone with a sedentary lifestyle.

3) BMR and PAL multiplied together give your daily energy requirement:

> Daily energy requirement (kcal) = BMR × PAL

4) You have to balance your energy intake to maintain a healthy weight:
- If you consume more energy than you use you will gain weight.
- If you consume less energy than you use you will start to lose weight.

CGP editor
PAL = about 1.6

5) This energy balance changes throughout life — for example:
- As you get older your BMR decreases, so you'll need fewer calories to maintain a healthy weight.
- As you exercise more your PAL increases, so you'll need more calories to maintain a healthy weight.

## Have the Right Balance of Energy Sources

Carbohydrates, fats and proteins are our main sources of energy.

According to government guidelines, they should be consumed in a certain ratio:

- Try to get a good variety, if eating low biological value proteins (p.1).

Carbohydrates 50%
Protein 15%
Fat 35% "or less"

- The majority should come as starches and as sugars present in milk (lactose) and fruit (fructose).
- No more than 5% should come from sugar added to processed foods.

- Getting less than 35% is fine.
- Try to eat less saturated fat.

## How to increase your PALs — go to lots of parties...

Know your BMR from your PAL and learn how to calculate how much energy we should consume each day.

Q1 How does obesity affect BMR? [2 marks]

Q2 Clive has a BMR of 2000 calories and a PAL of 1.5.
How many calories should he consume per day to maintain his weight? [1 mark]

# Nutritional Analysis

Nutritional analysis is about working out the nutritional content of foods... yup, this first bit is a little mathsy.

## Macronutrients *Have Different Energy Values*

1) Energy can be expressed in kilojoules (kJ) or, more commonly, kilocalories (kcal) — when people talk about calories in food, they're usually referring to kilocalories.

2) 1 gram of each major macronutrient (fat, protein and carbohydrate) gives us the approximate energy values shown in the table.

3) If you know how many grams of each macronutrient are in a food, you can calculate its energy value.

4) You can do this for an ingredient, a recipe and even a diet to work out the total energy value. For example:

| Macronutrient | Energy value (kcal) |
|---|---|
| Fat (1 g) | 9 |
| Protein (1 g) | 4 |
| Carbohydrate (1 g) | 4 |

To calculate the total energy value for a boiled egg with toast soldiers, look at the table to find the energy value for 1 g of each ingredient and multiply it by how many grams of each macronutrient there are.

| Ingredient | Macronutrient content | | Energy value | |
|---|---|---|---|---|
| 1 egg | Fat | 7 g | 7 × 9 = 63 kcal | 63 + 36 + 2.4 = 101.4 kcal |
| | Protein | 9 g | 9 × 4 = 36 kcal | |
| | Carbohydrate | 0.6 g | 0.6 × 4 = 2.4 kcal | |
| 1 wholemeal bread slice | Fat | 1 g | 1 × 9 = 9 kcal | 9 + 12 + 48 = 69 kcal |
| | Protein | 3 g | 3 × 4 = 12 kcal | |
| | Carbohydrate | 12 g | 12 × 4 = 48 kcal | |

Total energy = 101.4 + 69 = 170.4 kcal

## Use Reference Tables *and Software to Find Nutritional Data*

Fortunately, you won't have to calculate the energy value of each ingredient — there's loads of nutritional data available out there for both energy and nutritional values, you just need to know where to find it.

1) Packaged foods have to include nutritional labels on their packaging by law (p.65).

2) Reference tables of nutrients for different foods can be found in books or online:

• Foods are listed alphabetically or by food group.

• The nutritional values are usually given per 100 g or per portion of the food...

• ...which means you can't just use these figures as they are. E.g. if you use 10 g of garlic in a recipe, you'll need to divide the values in its row by 10 to give the nutritional value for just 10 g.

| Value per 100g | Energy (kcal) | Protein (g) | Carbohydrates (g) | Sugars (g) | Fat (g) | of which saturates | Fibre (g) |
|---|---|---|---|---|---|---|---|
| Garlic, raw | 150 | 6 | 30 | 1 | 0.5 | 0.1 | 2 |
| Gooseberries | 45 | 1 | 10 | 8 | 0.5 | 0.1 | 4 |
| Gouda, cheese | 350 | 25 | 2 | 2 | 28 | 18 | 0 |

3) You can also use nutritional analysis software on a computer:

• It lets you input the ingredients of a recipe, and the weight of each.

• It calculates the energy and the amount of nutrients present in the entire meal, and if the recipe serves multiple people, you can find the nutritional content per portion.

• It can have additional features such as comparing nutritional values to the recommended amounts for different ages.

"Explore food" is a free nutritional analysis tool you can try online — visit http://explorefood.foodafactoflife.org.uk/ for more info.

Mashed potato coats — the latest in food soft-wear.

# Nutritional Analysis

Whoopie — you can look up and work out the energy and nutritional information of foods... so what?
Well, armed with this data you can suggest and change ingredients to make meals more healthy and balanced.

## Modify Meals to Follow Healthy Eating Guidelines

Nutritional analysis helps you identify and adapt recipes, menus or diets to follow healthy eating guidelines.

Look at the ingredients in the recipe on the right.
Find the nutritional content of the recipe and modify
the ingredients to meet healthy eating guidelines.

The nutritional values of foods are often given in grams, so
estimate the weight of the lemon juice — 60 ml ≈ 60 g.

Use reference tables or nutritional analysis
software to find the nutritional values for each
ingredient, for the whole recipe and per portion:

E.g.

| Rhubarb Crumble | Energy (kcal) | Protein (g) | Carbohydrates (g) | Sugars (g) | Fat (g) | of which saturates | Fibre (g) |
|---|---|---|---|---|---|---|---|
| per recipe (~800 g) | 1708 | 16 | 258 | 106 | 68 | 42 | 10 |
| per portion (~200 g) | 427 | 4 | 64.5 | 26.5 | 17 | 10.5 | 2.5 |

The recipe serves four, so divide by four to get the nutritional values per portion.

**Rhubarb Crumble**
*(Serves four)*

Ingredients:
400 g rhubarb
100 g demerara sugar    80 g salted butter
150 g white flour    60 ml lemon juice

Modifying the recipe:

- Switch to a wholemeal flour to give the crumble more fibre and substitute 25 g of the flour for oats to give a better texture.
- The sugar content is really high — reduce the amount of sugar used to 50 g or use a natural alternative sweetener such as stevia or xylitol.
- Add a handful of walnuts to provide extra nutrients (unsaturated fats, fibre and vitamins).

Here are some ways you can modify recipes to reduce sugar, salt and saturated fat, and to increase fibre:

### Reducing Sugar
- Sugar can be 'disguised' as other names (e.g. sucrose, corn syrup) on packaging, so study labels carefully.
- Use fewer sugary condiments (e.g. ketchup, barbecue sauce).
- Use less sugar when baking.

### Reducing Salt
- Use less foods that have salt added to preserve or flavour them, e.g. cured meat.
- Create your own sauces and stocks — ready-made ones are often very high in salt.
- Use seasonings other than salt to add flavour, e.g. ginger or chilli.

### Increasing Fibre
- Go for wholemeal bread, flour and pasta.
- Include more beans, lentils (and other pulses) and vegetables in meals.
- Keep skins on potatoes.

### Reducing Saturated Fat
- Use low-fat spreads and vegetable oils.
- Eat lean cuts of meat, and grill, bake or steam foods instead of frying or roasting.
- Allow fat to drain away when cooking.

You also have to consider whether your meal is appropriate. A person:
- with a high PAL / about to take part in physical activity will require more energy in a meal.
- with a dietary requirement will require substitutions of certain ingredients (see p.20-21).

## Want some information on Bacon? Go to an art calorie...

Try experimenting with recipe ideas and use reference tables or software to find how the nutritional value varies.

Q1    Calculate the energy value of a pork pie (30 g fat, 15 g protein and 30 g of carbohydrates).    [2 marks]

Q2    Give three ways you could modify potato chips to make them more nutritionally balanced.    [3 marks]

# Planning Meals for Different Groups

There are many <u>factors</u> to consider when planning meals, e.g. <u>costing</u>, <u>portion size</u> and <u>dietary requirements</u>. You need to cater for different <u>ages</u> too — children might not rave about your <u>healthy cabbage soup</u>.

## Research the Cost of Ingredients

1) <u>Healthier</u> and more <u>nutritional</u> ingredients are often <u>more expensive</u> — e.g. <u>lean meat</u> (p.45).

2) Buying <u>individual</u> ingredients for a recipe is often <u>cheaper per portion</u> than buying <u>ready-made</u> food, e.g. a <u>pizza</u>. However, you'll usually have to buy <u>more</u> ingredients than you need for the recipe.

3) You can <u>compare</u> the prices of <u>ingredients</u> at <u>different shops</u> (or use <u>comparison websites</u>) and <u>reduce</u> the <u>quantity</u> of <u>expensive ingredients</u> (e.g. <u>cheese</u>, <u>meat</u>) to make your meals <u>cheaper</u>.

4) You can <u>work out</u> the <u>total cost</u> of a meal by working out the cost of each <u>individual ingredient</u> — <u>write down</u> each ingredient and <u>calculate</u> its <u>cost</u> from its <u>weight</u>:

| | Ingredient | Weight | Cost (per 100 g) | Cost (per ingredient) |
|---|---|---|---|---|
| **Spanish omelette (serves 4)** | Potatoes (500 g) | 500 g | £0.10 | £0.10 x 5 = £0.50 |
| | Butter (20 g) | 20 g | £0.40 | £0.40 ÷ 5 = £0.08 |
| | 2 Onions | 200 g | £0.06 | £0.06 x 2 = £0.12 |
| | 1 Red Pepper | 150 g | £0.50 | £0.50 x 1.5 = £0.75 |
| | 9 Eggs | 500 g | £0.30 | £0.30 x 5 = £1.50 |

<u>Total cost</u>
**£0.50 + £0.08 + £0.12 + £0.75 + £1.50 = £2.95**

<u>Cost per portion</u>
**£2.95 ÷ 4 = about £0.74**

## Control Your Portion Size

<u>Portion size</u> is <u>important</u> — good portion <u>control</u> means you can avoid <u>overfeeding</u> or <u>underfeeding</u> people. For ingredients and meals you may want to use <u>guidelines</u> and <u>equipment</u> to get the portion size correct:

<u>One portion</u> of <u>meat</u> should be roughly the size of your <u>palm</u>.

<u>One portion</u> of <u>cooked vegetables</u> should be roughly the size of your <u>fist</u>.

Use <u>scoops</u> to measure out the <u>same</u> portion size <u>each time</u>.

Use <u>cutters</u> and <u>dividers</u> to <u>divide</u> pizzas, pies, cakes etc.

## Meal Ideas for Different Age Groups

Make sure you plan your meals to be <u>nutritionally balanced</u>, <u>appropriate</u> for the <u>age group</u> (p.12-13) and that any <u>dietary requirements</u> (next page) are catered for. Take a look at these <u>examples</u>:

| | Ingredients | Nutritional importance |
|---|---|---|
| **Children** | Baked fishcakes | Good source of protein — children need lots of it. |
| | Carrots, peas | Packed with vitamin C (and make up 2 of their 5 a day). |
| | Mashed potato | A starchy carbohydrate that is a healthier alternative to chips. Made with milk so includes calcium needed for healthy teeth and bones. |

Make meals for children <u>visually interesting</u> by including different <u>colours</u> and <u>textures</u>.

| | Ingredients | Nutritional importance |
|---|---|---|
| **Teenagers** | Grilled chicken breast | Protein for rapidly growing bodies. |
| | Wholewheat couscous | Lots of carbohydrate and fibre and low in saturated fat. |
| | Olives, spinach | Both good sources of iron — important for girls so they don't become anaemic. |
| | Red pepper | Adds colour and a good source of vitamin C too. |

**EXAM TIP:**
You might have to modify a recipe to make it more nutritionally balanced — e.g. how could you increase the calcium content here?

| | Ingredients | Nutritional importance |
|---|---|---|
| **Elderly** | Lentil stew | Pulses are rich in protein and fibre. Fibre helps the weakening digestive system. |
| | Sweet potato | Lots of carotene (vitamin A) — helpful for healthy eyes. |
| | Soft tofu | Easy to chew and can be a good source of calcium to help maintain bone strength. |
| | Wholemeal bread roll | Another good source of fibre — much more than white bread. |

# Planning Meals for Different Groups

You may have to plan a meal for someone with a <u>dietary requirement</u> — <u>intolerances</u>, <u>allergies</u>, <u>ethical</u> and <u>religious beliefs</u>, and <u>diet-related health problems</u> all affect what people eat.

## Intolerances and Allergies

### Lactose Intolerance

People with <u>lactose intolerance</u> need to avoid food containing a type of sugar called <u>lactose</u>. Lactose is found in <u>milk</u>, so it's important to check labels for any <u>milk-based</u> ingredients.

* Consider <u>substituting</u> normal milk for <u>lactose-free</u> milk, e.g. <u>soya</u> or <u>almond</u> milk.
* <u>Dairy</u> products, e.g. cheese and yoghurt, have <u>lactose-free alternatives</u>.

Soya beans

### Nut Allergy

People with <u>nut allergies</u> have to avoid <u>nuts</u> and foods that may <u>contain traces</u> of them. <u>Allergic reactions</u> can be <u>fatal</u>, so it's important you check labels very carefully — if you have any doubts about whether a product contains nuts it's safest not to use it.

* Nuts <u>aren't vital</u> for a balanced diet, so <u>substitutions</u> can be made.
* Some <u>biscuit</u> and <u>cake</u> recipes only use nuts to add flavour, so the nuts can just be <u>removed</u>.

### Coeliac Disease

People with <u>coeliac disease</u> cannot eat food containing <u>gluten</u>. They must avoid <u>wheat</u>, <u>barley</u> and <u>rye</u> and products made with them.

* Many <u>basic foods</u> are fine for a <u>coeliac</u> — meat, vegetables and dairy products are all <u>naturally free</u> of gluten and should be included in their normal diet. However, you should check the label just in case.
* Use <u>alternative flours</u>, e.g. <u>coconut</u>, <u>tapioca</u> or <u>rice</u> flours are all <u>gluten-free alternatives</u> to <u>wheat flour</u>.

## Ethical and Moral Beliefs

See p.63 for more on ethical and moral beliefs.

### Vegetarians

A <u>vegetarian</u> is someone who <u>chooses</u> not to eat <u>any meat</u> (and sometimes <u>products</u> derived from <u>animals</u>, like milk and eggs) due to <u>personal</u> or <u>religious beliefs</u>.

Make sure you can plan meals for people with religious beliefs too (see p.62).

There are different <u>branches</u> of <u>vegetarianism</u>:

* <u>Pescatarians</u> will <u>not</u> eat <u>meat</u>, but <u>will</u> eat <u>fish</u> and <u>animal products</u>, e.g. eggs, cheese and milk.
* <u>Lacto-ovo</u> vegetarians will <u>not</u> eat any <u>meat</u> or <u>fish</u> but <u>will</u> eat milk, eggs and other <u>animal products</u>.
* <u>Lacto</u> vegetarians will <u>not</u> eat any <u>meat</u>, <u>fish</u> or <u>eggs</u>, but <u>will</u> eat milk and other <u>dairy products</u>.
* <u>Vegans</u> will <u>not</u> eat any <u>meat</u>, <u>fish</u> or <u>animal products</u>.

1) Dishes with vegetables are generally <u>healthy</u> and <u>nutritionally balanced</u>, but you will have to include protein from <u>alternative sources</u> than meat (see p.1).
2) <u>Quorn</u>™ products are popular — they contain <u>mycoprotein</u> which is said to have a texture similar to meat (most Quorn™ products use <u>egg white</u>, so they are not all suitable for vegans).
3) Be careful of hidden animal-based ingredients, such as <u>gelatine</u> (used in jelly and marshmallows) and <u>rennet</u> (used in cheese).

# Planning Meals for Different Groups

## Diet-Related Health Problems

See p.14-15 for more on diet-related health problems.

### Obesity and Cardiovascular Disease

People with obesity need to lower their calorie intake and amount of saturated fat.

- Use correct portion sizes to control the amount of calories in a meal.
- Reduce the amount of saturated fat by using vegetable oils when frying and opt for cooking methods that don't add extra fat (e.g. grilling).
- Include more fruit and vegetables to replace fatty and sugary foods.

Obesity is a risk factor of cardiovascular disease, so this advice should be followed for people with cardiovascular disease too.

### Diabetes

People with diabetes need to control their blood sugar levels.

- Avoid adding sugar or use natural sweeteners, such as xylitol and stevia.
- Use low GI foods (see p.5) such as brown rice or quinoa because these foods are digested slowly and gradually raise blood sugar levels.

Keen for some quinoa?

### Anaemia

People with anaemia need good sources of iron in their diet (and vitamin C to help the body absorb it).

- Include foods high in iron, e.g. red meat and dark-green leafy vegetables.
- Include foods high in vitamin C, e.g. tomatoes and citrus fruits.

### Bone Diseases

People with bone diseases (e.g. rickets, osteoporosis) need good sources of calcium in their diet (and vitamin D to help the body absorb it).

- Include foods high in calcium, e.g. milk, cheese and calcium-set tofu.
- Include foods high in vitamin D, e.g. tuna and salmon.

### Dental Caries

People with dental caries need to limit their intake of sugary foods.

- Use less free sugar in recipes or use natural sweeteners instead (some evidence suggests that the natural sweetener xylitol may help prevent dental caries).
- Offer fluoridated water or unsweetened tea or coffee with meals rather than sugary drinks, e.g. fruit juice or fizzy drinks.

---

## Snails, snakes, dolphins — all of them lactose...

By now you should be confident adapting recipes to make them suitable for different groups and know how to cost things correctly — alternative ingredients (e.g. gluten-free) can often be more expensive than regular foods.

Q1    Adapt these dishes to make them more suitable for each of the following:

    a) Cottage pie for someone with lactose intolerance.     [1 mark]

    b) Chicken and broccoli pasta bake for a vegetarian.     [1 mark]

    c) Cheese and bacon lasagne for someone with cardiovascular disease.     [1 mark]

# Revision Questions for Section One

That's your lot for <u>section 1</u> — make sure you go back to any tricky bits before delving into these questions.

- Try these questions and <u>tick off each one</u> when you <u>get it right</u>.
- When you've done <u>all the questions</u> for a topic and are <u>completely happy</u> with it, tick off the topic.

## Protein, Fats and Carbohydrates (p.1-6) ☑

1) Give three reasons our bodies need proteins. ☑
2) Describe the health problems caused by   a) an excess of protein     b) a deficiency of protein ☑
3) Name four 'alternative proteins'. ☑
4) Give three reasons our bodies need fats. ☑
5) Explain the difference between saturated and unsaturated fats. ☑
6) What are the functions of omega-3 and omega-6 fatty acids in the diet? ☑
7) Describe four effects caused by   a) an excess of fat     b) a deficiency of fat ☑
8) Describe three effects caused by  a) an excess of carbohydrates   b) a deficiency of carbohydrates ☑

## Vitamins, Minerals, Fibre and Water (p.7-10) ☑

9) For each fat-soluble vitamin, A and D:        a) Give an example of a food it can be found in
   b) Explain why the body needs it        c) Explain a risk of having a deficiency of it ☑
10) List five foods that are rich in B-vitamins. ☑
11) Explain the importance of the following vitamins in our diet:
    a) B1 (thiamin)    b) B2 (riboflavin)    c) B9 (folic acid)    d) B12    e) C (ascorbic acid) ☑
12) Explain the importance of these minerals in our diet:
    a) Calcium    b) Iron    c) Potassium    d) Magnesium ☑
13) Why is fibre needed for our digestive systems? ☑
14) Explain why it's important to keep the body hydrated. ☑

## Healthy Eating Guidelines and Nutritional Needs (p.11-13) ☑

15) Sketch and label each section of the 'Eatwell Guide'. ☑
16) Describe the nutritional needs for:   a) toddlers    b) teenagers    c) young adults    d) elderly adults ☑

## Diet-Related Health Problems (p.14-15) ☑

17) Describe the causes and health problems for the following:
    a) obesity        b) cardiovascular disease        c) anaemia        d) type 2 diabetes ☑
18) Explain what the following health problems are and how you could prevent them:
    a) rickets        b) osteoporosis        c) dental caries ☑

## Energy Needs, Nutritional Analysis and Planning Meals (p.16-21) ☑

19) What is:   a) basal metabolic rate (BMR)     b) physical activity level (PAL)? ☑
20) According to government guidelines, what percentage of our total energy should come from:
    a) carbohydrates        b) fat        c) proteins? ☑
21) What is nutritional analysis?  Where can you find nutritional data? ☑
22) Give one example of how you can modify a recipe to:
    a) reduce sugar        b) reduce salt       c) reduce saturated fat     d) increase fibre ☑
23) Draw a table that could be used to calculate the cost of a recipe. ☑
24) Give two examples of equipment used to control portion size. ☑
25) Plan a meal for each dietary requirement below.  Explain why you chose each ingredient.
    a) lactose intolerance    b) cardiovascular disease    c) coeliac disease    d) lacto-ovo vegetarian ☑

# Why Food is Cooked

We all love food — heck, we have at least three moments in the day dedicated to it.  This section explains <u>why</u> we cook food, the <u>different ways</u> we cook it and the <u>science</u> behind these methods — let's get started...

## Food is Cooked for Many Different Reasons

<u>Different cooking methods</u> change our food in <u>different ways</u> — these include changes to <u>sensory properties</u> (<u>appearance</u>, <u>texture</u>, <u>flavour</u> and <u>smell</u>) and changes to <u>nutritive value</u>.  Below are some of the reasons why we cook — keep them in mind as you read this section, as lots of the information relates back to these points:

### To make it safe to eat

1) Many food sources (including <u>meat</u>, <u>poultry</u> and <u>eggs</u>) can contain <u>harmful bacteria</u> that can make us ill.  Luckily, bacteria can be <u>killed</u> if food is cooked long enough at a <u>high temperature</u> (see p.38).

2) Some foods contain <u>harmful toxins</u> that are <u>destroyed</u> when the food is cooked — e.g. <u>red kidney beans</u> have to be soaked, boiled and simmered before they are safe to eat, crikey!

### To improve shelf life

1) When foods are cooked at high temperatures, <u>bacteria</u> and <u>mould</u> are <u>destroyed</u> (see p.38).

2) This is one of the ways that food can be <u>preserved</u> during the manufacturing process.

3) E.g. milk is <u>pasteurised</u> (heated to a high temperature and cooled) — this helps it stay <u>fresh</u> for <u>longer</u>.

### To develop flavours

1) <u>Chemical reactions</u> take place during cooking that <u>change</u> the <u>flavour</u> of the food.  E.g. <u>caramelisation</u> can occur when onions are cooked, making them taste <u>sweeter</u> (see p.30).

2) <u>Roasting</u> meats and vegetables creates more <u>intense flavours</u>.  The food becomes <u>browner</u> and <u>crispier</u> with more <u>fat added</u> to it and as <u>water evaporates</u> from inside the food.

3) Cooking also allows the flavours of <u>different foods</u> to <u>combine</u>, e.g. when braising a meat in a pot of <u>liquid</u> and <u>veg</u> (see p.26).

### To improve texture

1) Cooking usually makes it <u>easier</u> for us to <u>chew</u>, <u>swallow</u> and <u>digest</u> our food.

2) Some foods become <u>softer</u> when they're cooked.  E.g. vegetables like broccoli and carrots become <u>more flexible</u> and foods like rice and pasta swell as their <u>starch molecules soften</u> (see p.30).

3) Meats become more <u>tender</u> (softer, more succulent and easier to chew) as <u>solid fats</u> in the food <u>melt</u> and <u>proteins</u> in the food <u>denature</u> (see p.29).

4) Other foods become <u>firm</u> when they're cooked.  E.g. the <u>proteins</u> in egg whites <u>coagulate</u> (see p.29) — this turns the food <u>opaque</u> and more <u>solid</u>.

5) However, meats can become <u>tough</u> and egg whites <u>rubbery</u> if they are <u>overcooked</u>.

6) A change in texture can also make food <u>more pleasant</u> to eat — e.g. roast potatoes have a <u>soft centre</u> but a <u>crispy outside</u>, and baked bread has a <u>light-textured</u> inside but a <u>crusty</u> outside.

### To give variety in the diet

1) Foods can be cooked in <u>different ways</u> to create <u>variety</u>.

2) For example, if you had a craving for beef you could satisfy it with <u>grilled steak</u>, <u>roast beef</u>, <u>beef stew</u>, <u>pan-fried minced beef</u> for a spaghetti Bolognese or a <u>barbecued burger</u> to name only a few.

My vegetarian friend had this really bad nightmare...

## The Science of Food?  I think it's thyme to raise the stakes...

Changing the flavour, texture and smell of our food is all about making it more palatable (appealing) — if I had the choice between a delicious, tender roast chicken or a tasteless, tough one I know which I would choose.

Q1   Explain why chicken must be cooked before it is eaten.                    [2 marks]

# Heat Transfer

Now it's time for a page of hard-boiled science — it's all about the different ways we use heat when cooking.

## Heat can be Transferred in Three Different Ways

Food is cooked using heat energy. Transferring heat energy means moving it from one place to another — this happens in three different ways:

### Conduction

1) Conduction is the transfer of heat energy through the vibration of particles.

2) In a solid, the particles are held tightly together. So when one particle vibrates, it bumps into other particles nearby and quickly passes the vibrations on.

3) When a pan is placed on a hob, heat energy from the hob causes particles in the pan to vibrate more and gain heat energy.

Particles in the hotter part of a solid vibrate more

Particles collide and pass on their heat energy

Heat flows in this direction through the solid.

4) When these particles collide with nearby particles, they pass some of their extra heat energy on to them.

5) This process continues throughout the pan until the heat has passed all the way through.

6) When food is placed into the hot pan, heat energy is transferred from the particles in the pan to the particles in the food in a similar way until the food is cooked through.

7) Metals are good conductors of heat. This is why most pans are made out of metal — so energy from the cooker is quickly transferred to the pan and its contents.

### Convection

1) Convection is the transfer of heat energy through gases (e.g. air) or liquids.

2) When you heat up a liquid, the liquid near the heat source warms up faster.

3) The warmer liquid rises above its colder surroundings — like a hot air balloon does.

4) As the warm liquid rises, colder liquid takes its place.

5) This colder liquid is heated and when it starts to rise, colder liquid takes its place.

6) As this process continues, you end up with a circulation of fluid (convection currents) — after a while, this circulation of heat results in the whole fluid being heated.

7) Convection also occurs in ovens — hot air rises and cooler air falls in the same way.

cooler fluid

warmer fluid

### Radiation

1) Radiation is the transfer of heat energy through waves of radiation — it's like how radiation from the Sun heats up the Earth.

2) Unlike conduction and convection, there is no direct contact between the heat source and the food.

3) Cookers like grills and toasters use radiation to cook food.

4) They emit waves of radiation — when these waves reach the food, they are absorbed and heat the food up.

5) Microwaves use radiation to heat up the fat, sugar and water molecules in our food.

Bread being toasted. The glowing heating elements emit radiation.

## Metals are good conductors — but what about Henry Wood?

Rather than using these heat transfer methods separately, we often use a combination of them when we cook.

Q1     Explain the methods of heat transfer used to bring a pan of water to the boil.     [4 marks]

# Cooking Methods — Water-Based

I don't know about you, but all this talk of cooking is starting to make me feel just a tiny bit <u>peckish</u>...

## *Water is Used to Cook in Lots of Different Ways*

### Boiling

- Boiling involves cooking food by heating it in a pan of <u>boiling liquid</u>, usually <u>water</u>.
- The types of food that are boiled include: tougher cuts of <u>meat</u>, <u>potatoes</u>, <u>rice</u>, <u>pasta</u> and <u>veg</u>.

- It's quite a <u>harsh</u> method of cooking and can't be used on delicate foods because the bubbles would break up the food — <u>over-boiling</u> can also make foods like pasta <u>too soft</u>.
- Boiling is a <u>healthy</u> way to cook as <u>no fat</u> is added. However, if veg is boiled for too long, <u>colour</u>, <u>flavour</u> and <u>water-soluble vitamins</u> (see p.8) are <u>lost</u> in the water.
- Boiled food is often not as <u>tasty</u> / <u>attractive</u> as food cooked by methods like roasting.
- However, boiling foods in a small amount of water with a <u>lid</u> covering the pan uses <u>less energy</u> than other methods, e.g. roasting or simmering.

> When boiling, heat is transferred by <u>conduction</u> (from the pan to the liquid and through the food) and <u>convection</u> (through the liquid).

> You can use the water from boiled food to make a tasty and nutritious stock or gravy.

### Steaming

- Steaming means cooking food with <u>steam</u> from <u>boiling water</u> or <u>stock</u>.
- Foods you can steam include: <u>fish</u>, <u>rice</u> and <u>vegetables</u>.

- <u>No fat</u> is added and because there is <u>no direct contact</u> with <u>water</u>, the veg keep more of their <u>taste</u>, <u>texture</u>, <u>colour</u> and <u>nutrients</u> than if they'd been boiled — this makes it the <u>healthiest</u> way to cook. However, food may not have as much <u>flavour</u> compared to, say, <u>fried</u> or <u>roasted</u> food.
- Steaming is a <u>gentle</u> way to cook — so it's a good method for <u>delicate</u> foods such as fish, but not for tough meats.

> When steaming, heat is transferred through <u>conduction</u> (from the pan to the water and through the food) and <u>convection</u> (through the steam).

### Blanching

- Blanching involves <u>part-cooking</u> food in <u>boiling water</u> for a very short time before putting it in <u>cold</u> (or iced) <u>water</u>.
- The cold water <u>stops</u> the <u>cooking process</u> — this helps to preserve <u>colour</u>, <u>texture</u> and <u>vitamins</u>.
- Blanching can be used to <u>remove harsh flavours</u> in food, e.g. <u>raw onions</u> are blanched to give them a <u>milder taste</u>.
- Blanching foods like <u>tomatoes</u> and <u>almonds</u> makes their skins shrivel up, making the skins much <u>easier to remove</u>.
- It's also used to prepare <u>fruit</u> & <u>veg</u> for <u>freezing</u> (see p.37).

### Simmering

- Simmering is like boiling, but more <u>gentle</u> as the <u>temperature</u> is slightly <u>lower</u> than boiling point (but still higher than when poaching).
- It's a very common cooking method for <u>soups</u> and <u>curries</u>.
- Simmering <u>preserves</u> more <u>nutrients</u> than boiling.

### Poaching

- Poaching involves cooking food in a pan of liquid <u>below boiling point</u>, usually around <u>80 °C</u>.
- The types of food that are poached include: <u>eggs</u>, <u>fruit</u> and <u>fish</u>.
- Poaching is a <u>gentle</u> way to cook and it helps keep the food <u>tender</u>.
- Like with boiling, <u>nutrients</u> and <u>flavours</u> are transferred to the liquid, lowering the <u>nutritional content</u> and <u>tastiness</u> of the food.
- However, if food is poached in a <u>tasty sauce</u> (e.g. fish poached in a white sauce), the food can absorb <u>flavours</u> and give <u>variety</u>.

> When poaching, heat is transferred through <u>conduction</u> (from the pan to the liquid and through the food) and <u>convection</u> (through the liquid).

# Cooking Methods — Water-Based and Fat-Based

## Braising

- Braising involves <u>slowly</u> cooking food in an ovenproof pot that has the lid on and contains <u>liquid</u> (usually water, stock or wine) and often <u>herbs</u> and <u>vegetables</u>.
- Food is cooked in the covered pot by a mixture of <u>simmering</u> and <u>steaming</u>.
- It's a great method for <u>big</u> or <u>tough</u> joints of <u>meat</u> because the gentle cooking of the meat helps to <u>tenderise</u> it.
- Before meat is braised, it's usually lightly fried to <u>brown</u> and <u>seal</u> it — this helps to keep <u>juices</u> inside the meat and gives it a <u>caramelised</u> flavour (see p.30).
- The <u>flavours</u> from the <u>liquid</u> and any <u>vegetables</u> and herbs in the pot are also <u>absorbed</u> by the joint — tasty.

When braising, heat is transferred through <u>conduction</u> (from the dish to the liquid and through the food) and <u>convection</u> (through the liquid and steam).

## Frying Uses Hot Fat or Oil to Cook Food

When frying, <u>fat</u> or <u>oil</u> is heated to a <u>very high temperature</u>. Different types of frying use <u>different amounts</u> of <u>fat</u>:

Hot oil or fat can cause <u>serious burns</u>, and it's <u>highly flammable</u> — so using a large amount can be dangerous.

When frying, heat is transferred to the food by <u>conduction</u> (from the pan to the fat and through the food).

### Stir-Frying

- Stir-frying tends to be done in a <u>wok</u> (a large round-based frying pan) coated in a <u>small amount</u> of oil, making it pretty healthy.
- Stir-fried foods include <u>noodles</u>, <u>vegetables</u>, <u>tofu</u> and small pieces of <u>meat</u> and <u>fish</u>.
- Food cooks <u>very quickly</u> and needs to be <u>moved</u> around the wok all the time so it doesn't burn — because they're cooked quickly, <u>vegetables</u> keep <u>more</u> of their <u>nutrients</u>.
- Stir-fried meals tend to have <u>more vegetables</u> than meat (some use no meat at all), making them a <u>healthy option</u>.

Stir-frying and shallow frying both increase the <u>flavour</u> of food because some of the fat is <u>absorbed</u> by the food as it cooks. Foods like onions also <u>caramelise</u> when they're fried, making them taste <u>sweeter</u> (see p.30).

### Shallow Frying

- Shallow frying uses a frying pan coated in a <u>medium amount</u> of fat or oil.
- Shallow-fried foods include: <u>meat</u> (like chops, bacon and sausages), <u>fish</u>, <u>eggs</u> and <u>pancakes</u>.
- <u>More fat</u> is used when shallow frying than stir-frying, so it's a <u>less healthy</u> method of cooking. Solid fats in the food also <u>melt</u> into the pan as the food cooks, increasing the amount of fat in the pan even more.
- Shallow frying gives foods a <u>crispier texture</u> than stir-frying.

Another fat-based method of cooking is <u>sweating</u>. This method <u>releases moisture</u> from food, making it more <u>tender</u> and <u>sweet-tasting</u>. Sweating is most often used for <u>vegetables</u> such as onions, and uses a <u>small amount of oil</u> over a <u>low heat</u> — it's this low heat that allows the food to release moisture <u>without browning</u>. While the food is sweating, it's usually <u>covered with a lid</u> to help the moisture (in the form of steam) <u>circulate</u> around the food.

## Hey — you're really steaming through this...

One of the key things to remember is that the longer you cook using a water-based method, the more water-soluble vitamins (B & C) are transferred from the food to the water. This lowers the nutritional value of the food — not good.

Q1      Describe one method you could use to cook a tough piece of meat. Explain your choice.     [3 marks]

Q2      Explain the benefits of steaming over other water-based methods of cooking.     [3 marks]

# Cooking Methods — Dry Methods

Here are two more pages of <u>cooking methods</u> for you to sink your teeth into. These pages focus on the <u>dry methods</u> of cooking: <u>baking</u>, <u>roasting</u>, <u>grilling</u> and <u>dry frying</u> — is anyone else's stomach grumbling right now?

## Baking Uses Dry Heat to Cook Food

1) Baking cooks food using <u>dry heat</u>, usually in an <u>oven</u>.

2) Lots of different types of food can be baked, including:

   • <u>bread</u>, <u>pastries</u>, <u>cakes</u>, <u>pies</u> and <u>tarts</u>

   • <u>potatoes</u>

   • whole <u>fishes</u>, like sea bass or salmon

3) <u>Meat</u> is also baked, e.g. in meatloaf or casseroles, although <u>large pieces</u> of meat are usually <u>roasted</u> (see next page).

4) Because <u>hot air rises</u>, the <u>top</u> of an oven is often <u>hotter</u> than the bottom — that's why food cooks <u>quicker</u> on the top shelf than on the bottom shelf.

5) Modern <u>electric ovens</u> are usually <u>fan-assisted</u> (or "<u>convection ovens</u>") — they have a fan inside that helps to <u>circulate</u> the hot air around the oven. They're much more useful because...

   • food bakes more <u>evenly</u> because all parts of the oven are at a <u>similar temperature</u>.
   • the oven <u>heats up quicker</u> and your food <u>cooks quicker</u> — so they use <u>less energy</u>.

> Heat is transferred around an oven by <u>radiation</u> and <u>convection</u>, and through the food by <u>conduction</u>.

> Baking food like fish or potatoes inside foil helps to keep the moisture in, making them nice and tasty.

**Advantages**
• A <u>wide variety</u> of food can be baked.
• The outside of the food <u>browns</u> and <u>crisps</u> up, which <u>looks</u> and <u>tastes nice</u>.
• It's <u>quite healthy</u> because <u>no extra fat</u> is added, and solid fats in the food often leave as the food is baked.

**Disadvantages**
• Baking food can take a <u>long</u> time.
• Food can become <u>dried out</u>.
• It uses a lot of <u>energy</u> as it requires the oven to be kept at a <u>high temperature</u> for a <u>long time</u>.

## Fat Can Drip Off Food as It's Grilled

1) Grilling uses a <u>dry heat</u> at a <u>higher temperature</u> than baking or roasting to cook food.

2) As food is grilled, fats <u>drip out</u> of the food and the outside of the food becomes <u>golden</u> and <u>crisp</u>.

3) <u>Barbecuing</u> is similar to grilling, but heat radiates from <u>hot coals</u> and food is cooked at <u>lower temperatures</u> for <u>longer</u>.

4) You can grill many foods, such as: <u>smaller bits of meat</u> (like steaks and sausages), <u>vegetables</u> (like courgettes and aubergines) and <u>cheeses</u> (like halloumi or goats' cheese).

> When grilling, heat is transferred to food through <u>radiation</u> (heat radiation from a grill, or hot coals when barbecuing) or <u>conduction</u> (if using a griddle pan).

> In summer, we often grill food on a barbecue instead of "barbecuing" food in this slow way.

**Advantages**
• Food cooks <u>quickly</u> at a high temperature.
• It's fairly <u>healthy</u> as <u>no fat</u> is <u>added</u> and fat from the food <u>drips off</u> when cooked.
• Just like roasting and baking, the golden outside of the food <u>looks</u> and <u>tastes</u> nice, and can have a lovely <u>crispy texture</u>.
• Grilling on a <u>barbecue</u> gives food a <u>smoky flavour</u> which is very <u>popular</u>.

**Disadvantages**
• The <u>high heat</u> used when grilling can make it hard to cook the food <u>evenly</u>.
• It's easy to <u>burn</u> the food, or to end up with the outside cooked but the inside still <u>raw</u> — this could lead to food poisoning (see p.41).
• Handling both raw and cooked meat on a barbecue might lead to <u>cross-contamination</u> (see p.40).

# Cooking Methods — Dry Methods

## *Fat is Added to Food When It's Roasted*

1) Like baking, <u>roasting</u> uses dry heat from an <u>oven</u>.

2) Roasting is usually done at a <u>higher temperature</u> than baking, so foods cook and brown more quickly.

3) <u>Fat</u> is often added to the outside of the food, e.g. potatoes or veg, to help it <u>brown</u> and stay <u>moist</u>. Fat can be added or the fat that has melted from the food (e.g. chicken) can be put back on top — this is called <u>basting</u>.

4) Common types of food that are roasted include: <u>large cuts of meat</u> (such as a leg of lamb, a cut of beef or a whole chicken), <u>potatoes</u>, <u>vegetables</u> (e.g. root vegetables, peppers and onions) and <u>chestnuts</u> (on an open fire...)

> Heat is transferred around an oven by <u>radiation</u> and <u>convection</u>, and through the food by <u>conduction</u>.

| Advantages | Disadvantages |
|---|---|
| • Extra fat and a high temperature helps to <u>brown</u> and <u>crisp</u> the outside of food, which <u>looks</u> and <u>tastes delicious</u>.<br>• The fat from roasted meat can be used to <u>cook other food</u>, e.g. potatoes or fried bread.<br>• Roasted food can be tasty and <u>moist</u>.<br>• Roasting can produce meat with a <u>rare</u> (undercooked) centre, which a lot of people like. | • Roasted food isn't always that <u>healthy</u>, as extra <u>fat</u> is often added.<br>• Just like baking, it takes a <u>long time</u> to roast food and uses a lot of <u>energy</u>. |

> Only certain types of meat (e.g. beef steak) can be served rare because of the dangers of food poisoning and parasites (see p.38).

## *Dry Frying Does Not Use Added Fat*

1) Dry frying means cooking food in a pan <u>without fat</u> or <u>oil</u>.

2) You can dry fry foods that contain <u>natural fat</u>, e.g. <u>minced meats</u>, and <u>bacon</u>. As the food heats up, the fats inside the food <u>melt</u> into the pan and begin to cook the food.

3) <u>Nuts</u>, <u>seeds</u> and <u>spices</u> can also be cooked in this way, although this method is usually called "<u>dry roasting</u>". This helps to release oils and bring out more flavour in the food.

4) Using a <u>medium heat</u> is important at the start of cooking to allow the fats to melt <u>without burning</u> the food — when the fat melts, the temperature can be increased as the fat starts to fry the food.

> When dry frying, heat is transferred by <u>conduction</u> (from the cooker to the pan and also through the food).

| Advantages | Disadvantages |
|---|---|
| • <u>No extra fats</u> or oils are added, making this method <u>healthier</u> than other frying methods.<br>• Dry roasting can be used to give a more <u>distinct aroma</u> to <u>nuts</u>, <u>seeds</u> and <u>spices</u>. | • It takes <u>longer</u> than other frying methods to cook meat thoroughly, because <u>lower temperatures</u> are needed at the start.<br>• It can only be used for a <u>small range</u> of food types compared to other cooking methods. |

## *Time for a break — my brain is fried after all these methods...*

Ahhh, there's nothing quite like the smell of baking wafting through the house... Apparently, a good way to remember something is to associate it with a smell. So get cooking and revising — perfect.

Q1      Give one similarity and one difference between roasting and baking.      [2 marks]

Q2      Why is grilling vegetables considered healthier than roasting them?      [1 mark]

# Changing Properties — Proteins

I hope you like <u>eggs</u>, because they're a great way to look at the <u>functional</u> and <u>chemical properties</u> of <u>proteins</u>. <u>Functional</u> = <u>how</u> they change food, <u>chemical</u> = the <u>science</u> behind these changes. Let's get cracking...

## Proteins Denature *During Preparation and Cooking*

protein

Denaturation

Coagulation

1) Proteins (p.1) have a <u>complex structure</u>. When food is cooked, proteins <u>denature</u> — this means the <u>chemical bonds</u> holding their structure together <u>break down</u>.

2) The proteins <u>unravel</u> and their shape <u>changes</u> — in <u>most cases</u> this is <u>irreversible</u>.

3) Proteins can be denatured in different ways, including:
   * Physical <u>agitation</u> (e.g. whisking, beating and kneading)
   * Changes in <u>temperature</u> (e.g. heat)
   * <u>Acids</u> (e.g. lemon juice and marinades)

> Acidic marinades denature the protein in meat before cooking — this makes the meat more tender before it's even been cooked, and more palatable once it has been cooked.

## Denatured Protein Molecules Coagulate

1) Once they have been <u>denatured</u>, protein molecules collide with other protein molecules and <u>coagulate</u> (join together).

2) During this process, <u>water</u> becomes <u>trapped</u> between the protein molecules.

3) Coagulation also changes the <u>appearance</u> and <u>texture</u> of the food. E.g. egg white turns from a <u>see-through liquid</u> into a <u>white solid</u>, while steak becomes <u>brown</u>, <u>firmer</u> and <u>easier to eat</u> as you cook it.

4) However, if food is <u>overcooked</u> and coagulation happens too much, the protein <u>tightens</u>. This forces <u>water out</u> of the molecules, making it <u>dry</u> and <u>chewy</u>.

> When eggs are added to breadcrumb coatings and quiche mixtures, the process of protein coagulation helps hold everything together.

## Foams are Formed When Air is Trapped

1) <u>Foams</u>, e.g. <u>chocolate mousse</u> or <u>cappuccino foam</u>, form when <u>gas</u> becomes <u>trapped</u> inside <u>liquid</u>.

2) When liquids containing <u>proteins</u> are <u>agitated</u> (e.g. egg whites are whisked), the proteins inside the liquid <u>denature</u> — this causes them to <u>stretch</u> and <u>air</u> becomes <u>trapped</u> in the liquid.

3) When the proteins <u>coagulate</u>, this air becomes <u>trapped</u>, creating a foam.

4) However, <u>over-whisking</u> causes these new protein bonds to break — air escapes and the foam <u>collapses</u>.

5) Some foams form a <u>solid</u> structure when they are cooked, e.g. egg white foams become <u>meringues</u>.

## Gluten Allows Doughs to Stretch and Rise

1) <u>Gluten</u> is a <u>protein</u> found in <u>wheat flours</u> (e.g. those made from <u>wheat</u>, <u>barley</u> and <u>rye</u>).

2) It's <u>formed</u> when <u>water</u> is mixed with the <u>flour</u> to make <u>dough</u> and can be found in foods like <u>bread</u>, <u>pasta</u>, <u>cakes</u> and <u>pastries</u>.

3) Molecules of gluten are <u>coiled</u> — this means they are able to stretch and bend — this gives all doughs <u>elasticity</u> (stretchiness).

4) Doughs need to be <u>kneaded</u> to 'work' the gluten — this causes gluten strands to get <u>longer</u>, <u>stronger</u> and <u>stretchier</u>.

5) When it reaches a high temperature, gluten <u>coagulates</u> (see above) and the <u>dough stays stretched</u>. This gives foods like well-risen bread a <u>light</u>, <u>airy texture</u>.

> To get a well-risen loaf of bread, it's best to use <u>strong flour</u> because it forms more gluten than other types (e.g. soft flour, which is used more often in cake making).

## Indiana Foams and the Temple of the Whipped Egg White...

It might be ~~fun~~ helpful to draw a mind map of the ways proteins change during cooking — include changes to their chemical properties (e.g. molecules coagulate) and how this affects their functional ones (e.g. food becomes firmer).

Q1    Explain what happens to the protein in egg white when you fry an egg.    [4 marks]

# Changing Properties — Carbohydrates

For the exam you'll need to know about three ways in which carbohydrates change in food during cooking. If you need a quick refresher on carbohydrates before we get going, have a quick flick back to pages 5-6.

## Starch Gelatinisation Thickens Liquids

1) Gelatinisation helps to thicken foods that contain starch, e.g. sauces, custards and gravies.

2) When starch granules are first mixed with liquid, they become suspended in it — if you don't stir the liquid these granules will sink to the bottom.

3) When the granules are heated with water, the bonds between starch molecules start to break, allowing water molecules to enter. As water is absorbed, the starch granules swell in size and soften.

4) Between 62 °C and 80 °C, the starch granules burst open and release their starch into the liquid.

5) This release of starch causes the liquid to thicken. How thick the liquid becomes depends on the ratio of starch to liquid in the mixture — the higher the concentration of starch, the thicker the liquid.

6) When it cools, the liquid solidifies and a solid gel is formed — this is useful for making 'set' desserts like custards and lemon pie filling.

Custards can also be set using gelatine or by the process of protein coagulation (see previous page).

7) Gelatinisation also happens when you cook starchy foods like pasta and rice — they swell, soften and release starch into the water as they cook.

## Dextrinisation Occurs When Starch is Exposed to Dry Heat

1) When starchy foods such as bread or biscuits are cooked with dry heat, e.g. toasting or baking, the starch molecules in the food break down into smaller molecules called dextrins.

2) This breakdown is called dextrinisation and it gives food a browner colour and crispier texture as well as a different taste (imagine the difference in taste between bread and toast).

3) The longer the food is cooked, the more starch is converted into dextrin and the darker and crispier the food becomes.

Random fact:
The psychological phenomenon of seeing things in everyday objects (toast, for example) is called pareidolia.

## Sugar Caramelises When It's Heated

1) Sugar molecules break down when they reach a high temperature — this causes sugar to turn brown and change flavour. This process is called caramelisation.

2) The sugar goes through various stages — it changes from a very sweet, runny liquid, to a smooth caramel, and it eventually develops a hard, candy-like texture.

3) Caramelised sugar can burn very quickly, turning black, brittle and bitter to taste.

4) Caramelisation gives desserts such as an apple pie or a crème brûlée extra sweetness and colour.

5) Even savoury foods that contain sugars (e.g. onions) can caramelise. The sugars in the food are broken down and released, turning the food brown and adding sweetness.

## Tony Starch — saving the world one sauce at a time...

Blimey, there are some long words on this page! While it might be tempting to read over them quickly, it's important you can spell them correctly — especially gelatinisation, dextrinisation and caramelisation — lovely...

Q1    Describe how dextrinisation affects the sensory properties of food. [2 marks]

Q2    Describe what happens to starch granules when they are heated with water. [3 marks]

# Changing Properties — Fats and Oils

Fats and oils get a bad rap, but they're actually really useful for a variety of cooking situations...

## Fats and Oils Have Lots of Different Uses

### Aeration Means Incorporating Air

Oils don't trap air as easily as fats — oil-based doughs need something else to add air, e.g. baking powder (see p.33).

1) When fats such as butter are beaten with sugar (this process is called creaming) air becomes trapped in the mixture. This air makes the mixture fluffier and lighter in colour.

2) This aeration gives cakes a spongy and light texture when they're cooked.

3) Foods can be aerated in many different ways, e.g. whisking egg whites with a whisk or quickly beating ingredients with a spoon — there's more about this on p.33.

### Shortening Gives Foods a Crumbly Texture

1) When you rub fat into flour, you cover the flour particles with fat — this gives the flour particles a waterproof coating.

2) This coating prevents long gluten molecules forming when water is added to the flour.

3) This means the dough cannot become stretchy and baked goods like shortbread keep a 'short' (firm and crumbly) texture — hence the name shortening.

4) Shortening is also used when making filled pies and tarts — it's helpful because the base doesn't rise and forms a solid case.

5) Some fats are called 'shortening' — they have 100% fat content (contain no water) which helps stop gluten formation and prevents steam from raising the food.

Lucy was thrilled that her shortening had been successful.

### Plasticity Means Ability to Be Spread and Shaped

1) Fats have 'plasticity' — we're able to spread and manipulate them.

2) This is possible because fats contain a mixture of different triglycerides (see p.3). These different triglycerides all melt at different temperatures — so fats gradually soften over a range of temperatures rather than melting at just one.

Butter can be hard in the fridge, soft at room temperature and melty when it's heated.

3) The more plasticity a fat has, the easier it is to spread.

4) You'll remember from p.3 that unsaturated fats tend to be soft or liquid at room temperature, while saturated fats tend to be solid — this means that the more unsaturated fatty acids a fat or oil contains, the more plasticity the fat or oil will have (e.g. it will be easier to spread).

5) Plasticity is useful for a range of different reasons, including:

   • Decorating cakes with buttercream
   • Rubbing fat into flour to make shortened dough (see above)
   • Spreading butter on sandwiches and toast
   • Putting cream cheese on crackers

An example of taking vegetable fat spread literally...

6) Some vegetable fat spreads are marketed as being 'easy to spread'. This is because they contain a mixture of triglycerides with low melting points, meaning you can spread them as soon as you take them out of the fridge.

# Changing Properties — Fats and Oils

We're not quite done with fats and oils yet. Time for the grand finale — emulsions...

## Emulsification *Keeps* Oil *and* Water *in a* Stable Emulsion

1) Emulsions are formed when oily and watery liquids are shaken together (the droplets of one spread out through the other).

2) Milk, margarine and mayonnaise are all examples of emulsions.

3) Usually, oil and water don't mix together and so emulsions separate out again unless you keep shaking or stirring them — or use an emulsifier.

4) The molecules in an emulsifier have two different ends: one is hydrophilic (attracted to water) and the other is hydrophobic (repulsed by water).

5) When you add an emulsifier, the water molecules bond to the hydrophilic side and the oil molecules bond to the hydrophobic side. This holds the oil and water together in a stable emulsion, preventing them from separating.

6) Emulsions can either be oil-in-water (e.g. milk, mayonnaise, salad dressings) or water-in-oil (e.g. margarine, butter).

7) Egg yolks contain a natural emulsifier called lecithin (also found in soya) — this is used as the emulsifier in margarine and mayonnaise.

oil droplets
water

hydrophilic head
hydrophobic tail

Mayonnaise is a stable emulsion of egg yolk, oil and vinegar. When making stable emulsions, you need to ensure you add the oil or water gradually and that you mix the ingredients for long enough.

He started it

## You Can Use Emulsions *for Sauces* and *Salad Dressings*

1) Emulsions are often used as sauces (e.g. mayonnaise) and salad dressings (e.g. vinaigrette).

2) Hollandaise sauce is another example of an emulsion sauce — it's made from butter, water, egg yolks (the lecithin in it acts as an emulsifier) and lemon juice (for flavour).

3) Follow these steps to make a hollandaise sauce:

- Melt the butter in a pan.
- Mix the egg yolks and lemon juice in a bowl.
- Gently warm this mixture by placing the bowl over a pan of simmering water.
- Slowly add the melted butter to the mixture, constantly whisking as you do.
- Keep whisking the sauce until it's all mixed together smoothly.

Note to self: Hollandaise sauce does not go well with apple crumble...

When making any oil-in-water emulsion, e.g. a sauce or dressing, it's important to add the liquid and emulsifier first, before very slowly adding the oil/fat while mixing vigorously.

## *My milk carton started leaking — I was overcome with emulsion...*

That's it for the functional properties of macronutrients — phew. It's tricky stuff, but make sure you understand it.

Q1    Explain why shortcrust pastry doesn't rise when it's baked.    [5 marks]

# Raising Agents

Unless you're craving pancakes, a flat, dense cake is not a good thing — this is why we use raising agents. Raising agents add gas (to doughs and mixtures) which expands when heated to create the rise.

## Some Raising Agents Produce Carbon Dioxide...

Don't be fooled — this is no cereal...

**Chemical**

- When it's heated, bicarbonate of soda breaks down to produce carbon dioxide bubbles that expand to make the mixture rise.
- It has an unpleasant alkaline (soapy) taste, so it needs to be used with a strong flavour to mask it. This is why it's used in things like gingerbread and chocolate cake.
- Baking powder is a mixture of bicarbonate of soda (an alkali) and cream of tartar (an acid). A neutralisation reaction takes place when baking powder is heated which gets rid of the horrid soapy taste.
- Self-raising flours contain a mixture of plain flour and baking powder.

**Biological**

- Yeast is a biological raising agent used in bread dough.
- It's a microorganism (see p.36) that causes fermentation — a process that releases alcohol and carbon dioxide.
- Doughs containing yeast are often proved (left in a warm place to allow fermentation to take place).
- This stage is important because it's when the carbon dioxide is released and trapped in the dough, causing it to rise — fermentation stops during baking as the yeast is killed by the heat.
- When the dough is baked, the carbon dioxide expands, causing the bread to rise even more — any alcohol produced by the yeast evaporates at this stage.

Using too much of a raising agent can actually cause cakes to sink — see p.72 for more about sinking cakes.

## ...Others Add Steam or Air to the Mixture

**Steam**

- When you use a very hot oven to cook a mixture that deliberately contains a lot of liquid (e.g. batters, puff pastry and choux pastry), water leaves the mixture as steam. As the steam rises it raises the mixture up.
- As the water leaves, the food bakes and becomes more solid. However, it's important to keep the oven door closed or the cold air from outside will cause the mixture to sink.

**Mechanical**

- We can add air into mixtures with just a little bit of good old-fashioned elbow grease:
- Air can be folded into mixtures and doughs in two different ways:
  1) To "fold" a cake mixture, you carefully use a spoon or spatula to repeatedly pour the liquid mixture over itself — trapping air each time.
  2) Pastry doughs can actually be folded into layers,  trapping air in between the layers each time you fold.
- Beating is a more vigorous method where you use a spoon or fork to mix ingredients and quickly drive air into the mixture — e.g. beating eggs and sugar in a mixing bowl.
- Whisking is the same as beating, but you use a whisk instead.
- When you sieve flour, air becomes trapped between the individual flour particles.
- Air is also added when creaming, e.g. creaming butter and sugar, and between flour particles when you rub fat into flour (see p.31).

## Learn this stuff — it's the yeast you can do...

Unlike chemical agents which add gas during baking, yeast adds gas to dough before baking. Yeast isn't used in cakes very often because cake mixtures struggle to hold air for the time it takes for fermentation to occur.

Q1　Give two examples of mechanical raising agents.　[2 marks]

Q2　Explain why you would not use bicarbonate of soda to raise a plain sponge cake.　[2 marks]

# Uses of Microorganisms

Microorganisms (e.g. bacteria, moulds and yeasts) are tiny living things found in air, water, soil, on people... basically everywhere. While they tend to have a bad reputation, they can be pretty useful in food production.

## *Yeasts Make Drinks Alcoholic and Bread Rise*

Alcoholic beverages are made using the fermentation of yeast:

- During the fermentation process, yeast converts sugar into carbon dioxide and ethanol (also known as alcohol).
- For example, the sugars in grapes are fermented to produce wine.
- Sometimes the carbon dioxide is left to add 'fizz' to the drink (e.g. with most ciders), but it can also be removed.

The production of many varieties of bread relies on the properties of yeast as a raising agent.

- Yeast is added to flour and water to form a dough. Salt is added for flavour, but also to strengthen the gluten in the dough.
- With the ideal conditions for growth (see p.36), the yeast quickly starts to grow. The yeast ferments the sugar to produce carbon dioxide — this gas is what causes the bread to rise.

## *Moulds can be Added to Cheese*

1) The blue bits on blue cheese (e.g. Gorgonzola and Stilton) are due to the moulds that have been added.
2) The mould gives the cheese a creamy texture and a distinctive sharp, tangy taste.

Cheesy fact: Blue cheeses have a strong smell — this is caused by the same bacteria behind foot and body odour. Lovely!

## *Bacteria are Used in Yoghurt, Cheese and Fermented Meats*

Bacteria are added to pasteurised milk to make yoghurt:

- The bacteria ferment lactose (milk sugar) and produce lactic acid.
- The lactic acid acts on the proteins in the milk to thicken it and gives it a sour or tangy taste.
- Probiotics (live bacteria) are a supplement in some yoghurts which are said to give health benefits.

A similar process is used in the production of cheese (see p.56).

Lactic acid-producing bacteria are also used to make fermented meats such as salami and chorizo:

- Raw meat (usually pork or beef) is mixed with a combination of ingredients, including salt, sugar, flavourings and a 'starter culture' of bacteria.
- The bacteria ferment the sugar and produce lactic acid — this lowers the pH of the meat, causing the proteins in the meat to denature and coagulate, forcing water out of the meat.
- This low pH and lack of moisture makes it much harder for pathogenic bacteria to grow (see p.36) — meaning the meat is safer to eat for longer.

## *Some microorganisms ne-ferment to hurt you...*

There you have it — some marvellous uses of microorganisms. Once you're familiar with all these examples, give this question a whack, then head on over to the next page for some revision questions on this section.

Q1      Explain the role of bacteria in the production of tzatziki (a Greek sauce made with yoghurt).      [2 marks]

# Revision Questions for Section Two

Congratulations — you've reached the end of <u>section 2</u>.  There was a lot of science in there, so well done.
*   Try these questions and <u>tick off each one</u> when you <u>get it right</u>.
*   When you've done <u>all the questions</u> for a topic and are <u>completely happy</u> with it, tick off the topic.

## Why Food is Cooked and Heat Transfer (p.23-24) ☐

1)  Give five reasons why food is cooked. ☑
2)  Explain in terms of particles how heat is transferred by conduction. ☑
3)  Which would be the most suitable material for a frying pan: metal or wood? ☑
4)  Explain how convection helps a liquid or gas to be heated. ☑
5)  Which method of heat transfer is used when toasting a slice of bread? ☑

## Cooking Methods (p.25-28) ☑

6)  Boiling and steaming are two water-based methods of cooking.
    a) Which of these methods involves direct contact with food?
    b) Which of these methods produces the more nutritious food? ☑
7)  Explain why food is plunged into cold water during blanching. ☑
8)  Give one similarity and one difference between braising and poaching. ☑
9)  Give a benefit of poaching over boiling. ☑
10) Which fat-based method of cooking is most suitable for cooking pancakes? ☑
11) Explain the difference between grilling and roasting. ☑
12) List the advantages and disadvantages of these cooking methods:
    a) simmering    b) baking    c) stir-frying    d) roasting    e) dry frying ☑

## Changing Properties (p.29-32) ☐

13) Give three ways proteins can be denatured. ☑
14) Describe the process of protein coagulation and explain how it affects the texture of food. ☑
15) Explain how foam formation happens in whisked egg whites. ☑
16) What is the name of the protein that gives bread dough its elasticity? ☑
17) Explain how starch can be used to thicken cheese sauce. ☑
18) Name the process that makes biscuits browner and crispier when they're baked. ☑
19) Name and describe the process that takes place when sugar is cooked at a high temperature. ☑
20) What does the term 'aeration' mean? ☑
21) Explain how you can prevent gluten molecules from forming long strands. ☑
22) What is the name given to a fat's ability to be shaped? ☑
23) Explain how emulsifiers can be used to keep oil and water in a stable emulsion. ☑

## Raising Agents and the Uses of Microorganisms (p.33-34) ☑

24) What are the differences between bicarbonate of soda, baking powder and self-raising flour? ☑
25) Name one biological raising agent and explain how it can be used to raise bread dough. ☑
26) Explain how choux pastry profiteroles are risen by steam. ☑
27) Describe six ways you could mechanically incorporate air into a cake mixture. ☑
28) Describe how microorganisms are used in the production of:
    a) yoghurt    b) salami    c) cheese    d) bread    e) alcoholic drinks ☑

# Food Spoilage

Microorganisms can be useful in <u>food production</u> (see p.34), but <u>pathogenic</u> ones are right party poopers...

## Microorganisms *Grow in the Right Conditions*

Microorganisms, e.g. <u>bacteria</u>, <u>moulds</u> and <u>yeasts</u>, need <u>five conditions</u> to <u>quickly</u> grow and <u>multiply</u>:

1) A <u>warm temperature</u>
2) Plenty of <u>moisture</u> (water)
3) Plenty of <u>food</u>
4) The right <u>pH</u> (not too <u>acidic</u> or <u>alkaline</u>)
5) Enough <u>time</u>
    (In <u>ideal</u> conditions, bacteria split every <u>10-20 minutes</u>)

<u>Pathogenic</u> microorganisms can <u>spoil</u> food (make it <u>go off</u>) and cause <u>food poisoning</u>.

> Pathogenic means something that can produce disease.

Changing any <u>one</u> of these <u>conditions</u> will <u>slow</u> or <u>stop</u> the growth of microorganisms altogether. For example, you could:

- Use a <u>fridge</u> to change the <u>temperature</u> (see p.38).
- <u>Pickle</u> the food in <u>vinegar</u> to change the <u>pH</u>.
- Add <u>salt</u> — salt <u>absorbs water</u> (removes moisture) from the food, <u>drying</u> it out.

## High Risk Foods *Have Ideal Conditions* for Bacteria

1) <u>High risk foods</u> are <u>ready-to-eat</u> foods that, if not <u>stored correctly</u>, could grow <u>harmful bacteria</u>.
2) They satisfy points <u>2 and 3</u> above — they're <u>moist</u> and <u>high in protein</u> (protein = <u>food</u> for bacteria).

| High Risk Foods |
|---|
| 1) <u>Cooked meat</u>, <u>fish</u> and <u>poultry</u> |
| 2) <u>Dairy products</u> (<u>eggs</u>, <u>cheese</u>, etc.) |
| 3) <u>Gravies</u>, <u>stocks</u> and <u>sauces</u> |
| 4) <u>Shellfish</u> |
| 5) <u>Cooked</u> rice |

3) High risk foods have a <u>short shelf life</u> — you can't keep them for long, or the bacteria might multiply to <u>dangerous levels</u>.

> The shelf life of a food is the length of time it can safely be kept for.

4) You can sometimes <u>identify</u> when a high risk food is <u>spoiling</u> — e.g. meat going <u>slimy</u>, milk smelling <u>sour</u> or cheese going <u>mouldy</u>...
5) ...but often <u>pathogenic bacteria</u> leave <u>no signs</u> — <u>taste</u>, <u>colour</u>, <u>odour</u> or <u>texture</u> aren't affected.
6) You can check there are no <u>visible</u> signs of spoilage when <u>buying food</u>:
   - <u>Fresh meat</u> should be brightly coloured, firm and have a fresh smell.
   - <u>Fresh fish</u> should have shiny skin, red gills, clear eyes and smell clean or slightly salty.

## Double, double, spoil and trouble...

Microorganisms, such as bacteria, multiply much more quickly in the right conditions. Luckily, you're able to slow the rate at which they do so by changing one or more of the factors above.  Phew.

Q1    Explain, for each choice below, which food bacteria would grow more quickly in:

a)  Whole milk or powdered (dried) milk                                          [2 marks]

b)  A refrigerated pizza or a pizza at room temperature                          [2 marks]

# Food Spoilage

Fruit and vegetables <u>change</u> over time — e.g. <u>unripe</u> blackberries are <u>green</u> and <u>turn black</u> when they are <u>ripe</u>. This is the work of <u>enzymes</u>...

## *Enzymes are Biological Catalysts*

<u>Enzymes</u> are <u>special proteins</u> that act as <u>biological catalysts</u> — they <u>speed up</u> chemical <u>reactions</u>. You can see the <u>effects</u> of enzymes in many <u>fruits</u> and <u>vegetables</u>:

Ripening
enzymes

Eurgh, way too green...          ...aah, much better!

**Ripening**
- <u>Enzymes</u> in fruit cause them to <u>ripen</u>, which affects the <u>sweetness</u>, <u>colour</u> and <u>texture</u> of the fruit.
- E.g. <u>Unripe</u> bananas are <u>green</u> and <u>firm</u> — enzymes <u>break down</u> <u>starch</u> inside them, which makes the banana <u>softer</u> and <u>sweeter</u>.

Enzymes speed up reactions with oxygen ('oxidation')

**Browning**
- When you <u>slice</u> fruits (apples, pears etc.), the <u>oxygen</u> in the air will turn the fruit <u>brown</u> (oxidation). Enzymes inside the fruit <u>speed up</u> this process.
- Leaving some fruit (bananas, avocados etc.) to <u>overripen</u> will give them a <u>brown colour</u> too.

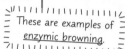

These are examples of <u>enzymic browning</u>.

## *You Can Slow or Stop an Enzyme from Working*

You can have some <u>control</u> over the <u>activity</u> of enzymes — here are a few <u>methods</u> that will <u>slow</u> or <u>prevent</u> the <u>unwanted</u> effects of enzymes:

VAT O' LEMON

- <u>Adding an acid</u> — enzymes <u>work best</u> at a <u>certain pH</u>. If you dip slices of fruit into <u>lemon juice</u>, the acidic conditions will <u>stop enzymic browning</u>.

- <u>Blanching</u> (plunging into <u>boiling water</u> for a short period — see p.25) is used to <u>prepare</u> vegetables for <u>freezing</u>. Natural <u>ripening enzymes</u> will cause veg to lose <u>colour</u>, <u>texture</u>, <u>flavour</u> and <u>nutrients</u> over time. Freezing will <u>slow down</u> the enzymes but not stop them completely. Blanching <u>destroys</u> the ripening enzymes, so the vegetables <u>retain</u> their colour, nutrients etc.

## *Mould and Yeast Can Spoil Food Too*

It was for a Science experiment, Mum! Honest!

1) <u>Moulds</u> and <u>yeasts</u> are both <u>microorganisms</u> (<u>fungi</u>) — this means in the right conditions (<u>warmth</u>, <u>moisture</u> etc.) they can <u>grow</u> and <u>spread</u> quickly.

2) Moulds spoil <u>bread</u>, <u>cheese</u> and <u>fruit</u> — they can change the <u>look</u>, <u>smell</u> and <u>taste</u> of the food. You can easily spot mould due to its '<u>fuzzy</u>' appearance.

3) <u>Waste products</u> from moulds can cause <u>food poisoning</u> — even if you <u>scrape</u> it off, <u>toxins</u> may still remain.

4) <u>Yeasts</u> commonly grow on the surfaces of <u>fruit</u>, e.g. <u>grapes</u>, <u>blackberries</u> and <u>tomatoes</u>, and spoil fruit by <u>fermenting</u> the sugars into <u>alcohol</u> and <u>carbon dioxide</u>.

5) Mould and yeast growth can be <u>prevented</u> by <u>correctly storing</u> food, e.g. storing <u>bread</u> in <u>dry, cool conditions</u> and most <u>fruits</u> in the <u>fridge</u>.

For wine production (see p.34) this 'spoiling' has a <u>desirable</u> effect.

## *A microorganism animated classic — 'Fruity and the Yeast'...*

Enzymic browning is usually an unwanted effect but it is useful for things like tea — different types of tea can be made by controlling the amount of browning on the tea leaves. Neat.

Q1    Identify one sign of food spoilage that could affect a tomato.          [1 mark]

Q2    Explain how brushing banana slices with lime juice affects enzymic activity.          [3 marks]

# Storing Food Safely

I like to eat food straight away — but some people out there like to <u>preserve</u> it. Where's the fun in that...

## *The Right Temperature is Vital to Storing Food Safely*

To <u>preserve</u> food, you need to keep it in <u>conditions</u> that <u>bacteria can't grow</u> in.
First up, there are some <u>critical temperatures</u> that affect bacterial growth:

### Cooking / Reheating (75 °C)

- Cooking food <u>above 75 °C kills</u> bacteria.
- It's important to <u>reheat</u> food <u>properly</u>, and <u>only once</u>. Reheat the food to above 75 °C for at least <u>three minutes</u>.
- <u>Check</u> food is at <u>least 75 °C</u> with a <u>temperature probe</u> (see p.40).

Since consumers won't usually have a temperature probe, manufacturers will often say 'check the food is piping hot' to make sure it gets cooked above 75 °C.

### Chilling (0 °C to 5 °C)

- Keeping food between <u>0 °C and 5 °C slows</u> down the growth of bacteria.
- This <u>extends</u> the <u>shelf life</u> of the food.
- Chilling food doesn't change its properties much — chilled food <u>looks</u> and <u>tastes</u> the same — but it may have a <u>harder texture</u>.

°C (thermometer: 80, 70, 60, 50, 40, 30, 20, 10, 0, −10, −20)

### The Danger Zone (5 °C to 63 °C)

- Bacteria grow and multiply <u>quickly</u> in temperatures from <u>5 °C to 63 °C</u>. This is called the <u>danger zone</u>.
- Hot food should be held <u>above 63 °C</u>.
- The <u>optimum temperature</u> for bacterial growth is <u>37 °C</u>.

This is your normal <u>body temperature</u>.

### Freezing (−18 °C)

- Freezing food below <u>−18 °C stops bacteria growing</u> — they become <u>dormant</u>.
- Freezing <u>greatly extends</u> the <u>shelf life</u> of the food and the <u>nutrients aren't lost</u>.
- It <u>doesn't kill</u> the bacteria though. They become <u>active</u> again when the food defrosts.

## *Use a Fridge and Freezer Correctly*

**Fridges**
1) Fridges should be <u>0 °C to 5 °C</u>, ideal for <u>chilling</u> foods (especially <u>high risk</u> foods).
2) Keep food <u>covered</u> or <u>stored in containers</u> to prevent <u>contaminating</u> other foods.
3) Don't let the <u>blood</u> and <u>juices</u> of raw meat <u>drip</u> onto other food — <u>always</u> store raw <u>meat</u>, <u>poultry</u> and <u>fish</u> on the <u>bottom shelf</u> in the fridge.

**Freezers**
1) Freezers are set at around <u>−18 °C</u>.
2) Food should have <u>clear labels</u> with the <u>date</u> they were frozen.
3) <u>Defrost</u> meat and poultry <u>thoroughly</u> in a <u>fridge</u> — if food is <u>partially frozen</u> the recommended <u>cooking time</u> may not be sufficient to <u>kill bacteria</u>...
4) ...or if <u>cooking from frozen</u>, follow the '<u>cook from frozen</u>' time.

You should also not overstock a fridge or freezer — air can't circulate so heat can't be removed efficiently.

<u>Freezers</u> and <u>frozen foods</u> use a <u>star rating</u> to indicate how long to <u>store</u> food:

| Storing in an ice box / freezer compartment of a fridge: | Storing in a domestic freezer: |
|---|---|
| * 1 week (−6 °C) | *** 3 months (−18 °C) |
| ** 1 month (−12 °C) | **** Until 'best before' end date on frozen foods (−18 °C or colder) |

## *Frying through the danger zone...*

Temperature control is really important, so make sure you can recall all of the critical temperatures above. Now, take a look at this immaculately drawn fridge on the left...

Q1   Explain whether the food in the fridge has been stored correctly.   [2 marks]

Q2   Sean cooks the beef and places the leftovers back in the fridge.
Explain the benefit of refrigerating the cooked beef.   [2 marks]

Section Three — Food Spoilage

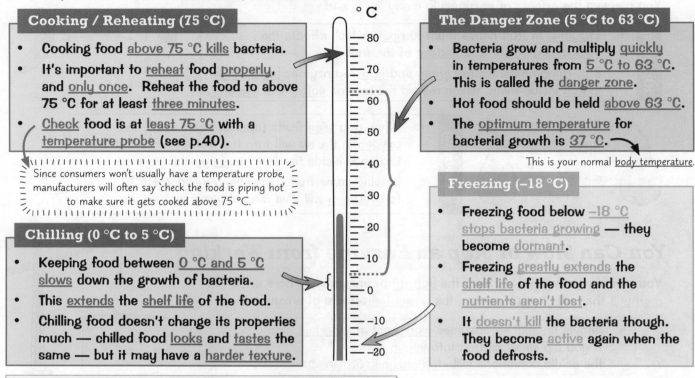

# Storing Food Safely

<u>Temperature control</u> is vital for <u>storing</u> food, so labels on food packaging will tell you whether you need to store it in a <u>fridge</u>, a <u>freezer</u> or just a '<u>cool, dry place</u>'. (There's other information on labels too — see p.64.)

## Some Food can be Kept in a Cool and Dry Place

1) Lots of food we buy from a <u>supermarket</u> doesn't need to be stored in a <u>fridge</u> or <u>freezer</u>.

2) Instead, they can be safely stored in a <u>cool</u>, <u>dry</u> place in their <u>original packaging</u> or an <u>airtight container</u>.

3) These foods contain little <u>moisture</u> or have been <u>processed</u> and <u>preserved</u> to make the conditions <u>difficult</u> for microorganisms to grow. These methods include:

> Foods that are kept at room temperature are also called <u>ambient</u> foods.

- <u>Freeze-drying</u> — food is frozen and dehydrated to remove <u>moisture</u> from the food (e.g. instant <u>coffee</u>).

- <u>Canning/bottling</u> — food is sealed in a <u>can</u> or <u>jar</u> and <u>heated</u> to kill off microorganisms.

- <u>Vacuum packing</u> — food is put into <u>plastic packaging</u>, and the air is <u>sucked out</u>.
  <u>Some</u> microorganisms can't survive without <u>oxygen</u>.

- <u>Pickling</u> — food (e.g. <u>gherkins</u>, <u>onions</u>) is plunged in <u>brine</u> or <u>vinegar</u>, making it too <u>acidic</u> for microorganisms to grow quickly.

- <u>Jam-making</u> — fruit is <u>boiled</u> with <u>sugar</u> and <u>pectin</u>, and sealed in a glass <u>jar</u> (see p.56). The <u>high sugar content</u> prevents microorganism growth.

Stu's soup was a little too tightly sealed.

4) These methods give foods a longer <u>shelf life</u> and make them safe to eat for many <u>months</u> or <u>years</u>.

## Don't Let Food Go Past Its Best

All food will eventually <u>spoil</u> or lose its <u>quality</u> — <u>date marks</u> must be <u>printed</u> on the <u>packaging</u> of the food you buy to help you know when the food is <u>likely</u> to be unsafe to eat or not taste <u>as good</u>.

### Use By Date

- The '<u>use by</u>' date is shown on products with a <u>short shelf life</u>, e.g. <u>high risk foods</u>.
- It's given as a <u>safety warning</u>. If you use the food <u>after</u> this date, it might <u>not be safe</u> — you run the risk of getting food poisoning.

| Keep refrigerated | |
|---|---|
| Cost | Use By |
| £2.50 | 24 JUN |

### Best Before Date

- The '<u>best before</u>' date is shown on products with a <u>longer shelf life</u>, e.g. <u>tinned foods</u>.
- It's given as a <u>warning</u> about <u>quality</u>. If you eat the food <u>after</u> this date, it's probably safe but might not be as nice as you'd expect, e.g. biscuits could be <u>soft</u>.
- <u>Eggs</u>, however, are <u>risky</u> to eat after their best before date — <u>salmonella bacteria</u> (see p.41) may have <u>multiplied</u> to <u>dangerous levels</u>.

BEST BEFORE
08-02-17
Store in a cool, dry place.

Groovy Beans

Food might be <u>OK</u> a bit after its best before date, but it won't be fine <u>forever</u>.
A <u>tin of baked beans</u> from the <u>1960s</u> is <u>probably not</u> going to be very nice on your <u>toast</u>.

## GCSE Revision — [Best Before: day of exam]...

There's a key difference between 'use by' and 'best before' dates — make sure you remember that 'use by' dates are about <u>food safety</u> and 'best before' dates are about <u>food quality</u>. Good. Let's crack on with some questions.

Q1 Explain how you would store a bag of dried pasta. [2 marks]

Q2 Explain which type of date mark will be on the packaging of raw poultry in a supermarket. [2 marks]

# Preparing Food Safely

If people eat food that's <u>contaminated</u> they could become very ill, so it's mega important that you handle food <u>safely</u> and <u>hygienically</u> to prevent bacteria spreading around the kitchen.

## *Avoid Cross-Contamination*

When working with food, it's really easy to <u>pass bacteria</u> from <u>raw food</u> to <u>work surfaces</u>, <u>equipment</u> and your <u>hands</u>. Bacteria are then easily transferred to <u>other food</u> — this is called <u>cross-contamination</u>.

<u>Cross-contamination</u> can happen from a <u>variety</u> of <u>different sources</u>:

- <u>Other contaminated food</u> — raw meat juices can drip onto cooked food.
  High risk foods such as gravy can contaminate lower risk foods when added to a meal.
- <u>Utensils, equipment and work surfaces</u> — using unclean equipment, dirty cloths on work surfaces or the same work surface / chopping board for raw meat and ready-to-eat foods.
- <u>People</u> — poor personal hygiene (especially unclean hands) and sneezing or coughing.
- <u>Pests</u> — flies, rodents etc. contaminate food directly by walking over / eating it  or by laying eggs and droppings on work surfaces. Waste bins will attract pests.

## *Follow Safety and Hygiene Procedures*

You should take steps to <u>reduce</u> the <u>risks</u> when <u>preparing</u>, <u>cooking</u> and <u>serving</u> food:

**Preparing**
- Follow <u>personal hygiene procedures</u> — <u>wash your hands</u>, wear a clean <u>apron</u>, wear a <u>hat</u> or <u>hair net</u> to cover your hair, remove all <u>jewellery</u>, cover all <u>cuts</u>.
- <u>Separate</u> raw and cooked foods and use <u>coloured chopping boards</u> for different food groups, e.g. you could use red for <u>raw meat</u> and brown for <u>raw vegetables</u>.
- <u>Wash raw vegetables</u> thoroughly — even traces of <u>soil</u> contain bacteria.
- Use <u>clean equipment</u> and an <u>antibacterial spray</u> to <u>sanitise</u> work surfaces.
- <u>Defrost</u> frozen food <u>fully</u>, in the bottom of a <u>fridge</u> and away from other food.

**Cooking**
- Cook food at the <u>right temperatures</u> (see p.38) and for <u>the correct time</u>.
- Make sure food is <u>cooked all the way through</u> — e.g. cook <u>thicker</u> pieces of meat for <u>longer</u> than thin ones.
- Test the temperature <u>inside</u> food using a temperature <u>probe</u>.

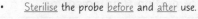

- <u>Sterilise</u> the probe <u>before</u> and <u>after</u> use.
- Insert it into the <u>middle</u> of the <u>thickest</u> part of the food.
- Leave the probe in until the temperature <u>stabilises</u>.
- Check that the probe reaches at <u>least 75 °C</u>.

**Serving**
- Serve hot food <u>straight away</u> or keep it above <u>63 °C</u> for no longer than <u>2 hours</u>.
- If you're serving food <u>cold</u> or <u>storing</u> it, cool it down <u>within 90 minutes</u>.
- Keep food <u>covered</u> to prevent <u>flies</u> or other <u>pests</u> contaminating it — preferably put it in the <u>fridge</u>.
- Try to avoid <u>wasting food</u>, and check that waste bins are not <u>overfilled</u>.

## *I wouldn't cross with contamination if I were you...*

It's dead easy for cross-contamination to happen. You have to be <u>very</u> careful and hygienic in the kitchen — especially if you're dealing with high risk foods that bacteria just lurrrveee.

Q1    Explain how each of the following is a food safety risk:

    a) Preparing all meals on one chopping board.                                                    [2 marks]

    b) Allowing my pet cats Mylo and Ziggy on the kitchen work surfaces.                  [2 marks]

# Food Poisoning

Hope you're not eating your lunch... it's time to take a peek at the most common <u>types</u> of <u>bacteria</u> that cause <u>food poisoning</u> and their (rather unpleasant) <u>symptoms</u>.

## Bacteria Can Cause *Food Poisoning*

1) The <u>general symptoms</u> of food poisoning include <u>sickness</u>, <u>diarrhoea</u>, <u>stomach cramps</u> and <u>fever</u>. In extreme cases, especially where people are <u>old</u>, <u>very young</u> or <u>vulnerable</u>, it can lead to <u>death</u>.

2) You can get food poisoning by eating <u>contaminated</u> food containing <u>pathogenic bacteria</u> — it can take a <u>few hours</u> to <u>several days</u> before you get any <u>symptoms</u>.

3) There are <u>many different</u> types of bacteria — you need to <u>learn</u> some of the <u>common</u> ones...

## Remember *These Main Types* of Bacteria

### Salmonella

- Found in <u>raw poultry</u>, untreated <u>milk</u> and <u>eggs</u>.
- Symptoms include <u>diarrhoea</u>, <u>stomach cramps</u> and <u>vomiting</u>.
- <u>Onset time</u>: 6–72 hours.

> Onset time is the time it takes from ingesting the bacteria to when symptoms first appear.

### Campylobacter

- The <u>most common</u> cause of <u>food poisoning</u> in the UK.
- Found mainly in <u>raw or undercooked poultry</u>, but also in other <u>raw meat</u>, and untreated <u>milk</u> / <u>water</u>.
- Symptoms include (bloody) <u>diarrhoea</u>, <u>stomach cramps</u> and <u>fever</u>.
- <u>Onset time</u>: 2–5 days.

> Who you calling a squid, punk?

### E. coli O157

- E. coli live in the <u>intestines</u> of <u>animals</u> and can contaminate <u>raw beef</u>, untreated <u>milk</u> / <u>water</u>, unwashed <u>vegetables</u> and <u>salad leaves</u>.
- Most types are <u>harmless</u> but <u>E. coli O157</u> can cause <u>kidney damage</u> and <u>death</u>.
- <u>Onset time</u>: 1–3 days.

### Staphylococcus aureus

- S. aureus live on the <u>skin</u> and <u>hair</u>, and in the <u>noses</u> of <u>animals</u> and <u>people</u>.
- <u>Poor personal hygiene</u> can <u>contaminate</u> food.
- Symptoms include <u>diarrhoea</u>, <u>stomach cramps</u>, <u>vomiting</u> and <u>mild fever</u>.
- <u>Onset time</u>: 1–6 hours.

> 'S. aureus' ends in 'us' — so it's easy to remember that you can find it in humans.

## Controlling Bacteria

Two <u>common foods</u> that could be contaminated with bacteria are <u>untreated milk</u> and <u>eggs</u>, so there are <u>methods</u> in place to make these foods <u>safe</u> for us to eat:

- <u>Pasteurisation</u> — all milk sold in supermarkets is <u>pasteurised</u>. Milk is <u>heated</u> at around <u>72 °C for 15 seconds</u> to kill off any <u>pathogenic</u> bacteria before being <u>chilled</u>.
- <u>Vaccinations</u> — the <u>British Lion Quality</u> mark on egg shells and boxes is for hens that have been vaccinated against <u>salmonella</u>, so that it doesn't contaminate their <u>eggs</u>.

---

## *I just can't stand salmonella, ella, ella...*

There are some big, scary names for these bacteria — you'll need to learn how to <u>spell</u> them (it took me a good 10 minutes to spell ~~Staffylowcouscous~~ Staphylococcus aureus) and the <u>key facts</u> about each.

Q1    Explain how a chef can reduce the risk of salmonella when preparing a dish containing eggs.    [3 marks]

# Revision Questions for Section Three

I'm sorry once again if section 3 put you off your lunch, but all that chat about bacteria is almost over... last thing to do is to tuck into these revision questions I've handpicked especially just for you.

- Try these questions and tick off each one when you get it right.
- When you've done all the questions for a topic and are completely happy with it, tick off the topic.

## Food Spoilage (p.36-37) ☑

1) What is a pathogenic microorganism?
2) Which five conditions are needed for the growth of microorganisms?
3) What is a high risk food? List five types of food that would be classed as high risk.
4) How do ripening enzymes change the properties of fruit and vegetables?
5) Explain what enzymic browning is.
6) Rhea is preparing a fruit salad. She says she can preserve it using lemon juice.
   Explain how lemon juice would help her preserve the fruit salad.
7) How can you prevent mould and yeast growth on fruit?

## Storing & Preparing Food Safely (p.38-40) ☑

8) Give the temperature, or range of temperatures, at which you would:
   a) reheat food
   b) chill food
   c) freeze food
9) What is meant by the danger zone?
10) How does freezing affect the shelf life of food?
11) What is the correct way of storing uncooked meat in a refrigerator?
12) Describe five methods that can be used to preserve and extend the shelf life of food.
13) How is a 'use by' date different from a 'best before' date?
14) What is 'cross-contamination'? List four possible sources of it.
15) Write a set of instructions to explain how to use a temperature probe correctly.
16) Delphine is making beef bourguignon — a stew prepared with braised beef.
    Give three safety steps she should take for each of these stages:
    a) preparing the beef bourguignon
    b) cooking the beef bourguignon
    c) serving the beef bourguignon

## Food Poisoning (p.41) ☑

17) List four general symptoms of food poisoning.
18) For each type of bacteria, say where it can be found:
    a) Salmonella
    b) Campylobacter
    c) E. coli
    d) Staphylococcus aureus
19) What is the 'onset time'? Which type of bacteria has an onset time of less than 6 hours?
20) Name two types of bacteria that could be found in raw minced beef.
21) Explain the process of milk pasteurisation.
22) How can you spot eggs from hens vaccinated against salmonella?

# Grown Food

This <u>section</u> is all about where your food <u>originally comes from</u> — it can be <u>grown</u>, <u>reared</u> or <u>caught</u>.

## Crops are Grown Intensively or Organically

<u>Grown food</u> includes <u>fruits</u>, <u>vegetables</u> and <u>cereals</u>, e.g. wheat, rice, barley, oats, rye.  There are two methods of farming them which you need to know about — <u>intensive farming</u> and <u>organic farming</u>.

### Intensive Farming Uses Chemicals to Achieve Maximum Yields

<u>Intensive farming</u> uses methods that will produce the <u>highest possible yield</u> (more food from the same area of land).  Production is often <u>large-scale</u>, with huge areas all growing the <u>same</u> crop.

1)  <u>Large mechanical equipment</u> is used to <u>save time</u> and <u>cut down</u> on <u>production costs</u>.

Intensive farming is also known as <u>conventional farming</u>.

2)  <u>Artificial (chemical) fertilisers</u> are added to the soil to <u>supply nutrients</u> for crops to grow.

3)  <u>Pesticides</u> are used.  These are <u>chemicals</u> that <u>control pests</u> and <u>protect</u> crops and include <u>insecticides</u>, <u>herbicides</u> (<u>weedkiller</u>) and <u>fungicides</u>.

4)  Some people are <u>concerned</u> about using artificial <u>fertilisers</u> and <u>pesticides</u>. They can harm <u>wildlife</u>, damage the environment, e.g. by <u>polluting rivers</u>, and some think they have a harmful effect on <u>human health</u> too.

Get outta my grub!

### Organic Farming Uses Natural Methods

Organic food is grown naturally <u>without</u> using artificial fertilisers and pesticides. This makes it more <u>expensive</u> to produce.

1)  Farmers add <u>organic matter</u> like <u>manure</u> and <u>compost</u> instead of artificial fertilisers.

2)  Techniques such as <u>crop rotation</u> (growing different crops) and leaving land <u>fallow</u> (growing nothing) are used to make sure the soil is <u>fertile</u> every <u>year</u>.

3)  Some farmers may use <u>alternative methods</u> to control pests.  Things like:

- Introducing a pest's <u>natural predators</u> (e.g. ladybirds to eat aphids).
- <u>Biological pesticides</u> (e.g. certain fungi).
- Spraying crops with <u>hot water</u>.

4)  These alternatives are generally <u>better</u> for the <u>environment</u>, but can be <u>more expensive</u> and <u>less effective</u> than using chemical pesticides.

5)  Organic farming has its share of <u>advantages</u> and <u>disadvantages</u>:

**Advantages**
- It <u>reduces</u> the amount of <u>chemical pesticides</u> going onto the land, so it's <u>less harmful</u> to the <u>environment</u>.
- Fewer <u>non-renewable resources</u> are used than in intensive farming, so it's more <u>sustainable</u>.
- It <u>appeals</u> to <u>consumers</u> (see p.63) who are <u>concerned</u> about the use of artificial <u>chemicals</u> and their damage to the <u>environment</u>.

**Disadvantages**
- Organic farming tends to produce a <u>lower yield</u>.
- There are higher <u>production costs</u>, which mean <u>higher prices</u> in <u>supermarkets</u>.

## Intensive farming is a load of crop...

There are advantages and disadvantages for both intensive and organic farming — you should be able to discuss how crop yields, production costs and environmental impact differ between these two farming methods.

Q1    Describe the methods used in intensive farming and the environmental impact they have.        [3 marks]

# Grown Food — GM Crops

People today are very concerned about how their food is produced and what effect it has on the environment. Organic foods are very popular, while lots of people are wary of GM foods.

## Genetically Modified Foods Have Altered Genes

1) A genetically modified (GM) food is one that's had its genes altered to give it useful characteristics, such as improving its growth or changing its colour:

> • GM plants are produced by inserting a desirable gene from another plant, an animal or a bacterium into the plant you want to improve.
> • You plant modified seeds and up comes your GM crop.

2) For example, you can get GM maize that's pest-resistant. The farmer gets a bigger yield of maize because less of the crop is eaten or damaged by pests.

3) GM weedkiller-resistant crops can withstand chemicals that kill the weeds around the crop.

4) Currently, no GM crops are grown in the UK, but it's popular in other countries, e.g. the USA grows lots of GM maize, cotton and soya beans.

5) GM foods have both advantages and disadvantages:

### Advantages

1) Crops can be made to grow quicker.
2) Producers can get higher yields of crops for the same amount of seed and fertiliser.
3) This makes food cheaper to produce so it's also cheaper for the consumer to buy.
4) Crops can be altered to have a longer shelf life — so less food is wasted.
5) Crops can be made to ripen earlier than normal, so fresh foods can be available for consumers earlier in the year.
6) Crops can be modified to contain extra nutrients which can improve nutrition in poor countries. E.g. golden rice has been genetically modified to contain carotene (which provides vitamin A).

### Disadvantages

1) GM foods haven't been around for long — so their long-term health effects aren't known.
2) There are concerns that modified genes could get out into the wider environment and cause problems, e.g. the weedkiller-resistance gene could be transferred to a weed, making it an indestructible 'superweed'.
3) GM producers can't sell their food everywhere — the European Union (EU) restricts the import of some GM foods.

## Consumers Have Safety Concerns

1) Some people believe that we shouldn't mess about with genes because it's not natural.

2) In the European Union:

> • All GM foods must undergo strict safety assessments and can only be sold if no health risks have been identified.
> • All foods that are GM or contain more than 1% GM ingredients must be clearly labelled.
> • However, meat and dairy products from animals fed on GM feed are not labelled.

## Gene E — altered to give farmers three wishes...

No, you can't wish for more wishes — that's not allowed. Genetic modification is a fairly new technology which can help food producers and consumers — but not everyone is convinced that the benefits outweigh the risks.

Q1    Give a reason why a crop might be genetically modified.    [1 mark]

Q2    Give two reasons why some people are against GM products.    [2 marks]

# Reared Food

Reared animals are animals raised by humans specifically for their meat (and other products).
E.g. cows are reared for beef and milk, and poultry (birds) for meat and eggs.

## Factory-Farmed Animals Don't Have Much Space

Factory-farmed animals don't have much room to move — they may be in cages with lots
of other animals in the same place. This is another form of intensive farming.

1) Animals are kept inside in warm sheds, so they don't waste much energy moving or keeping
   themselves warm. That means that more of their energy goes into producing meat or eggs for food
   — this maximises food production.

2) Animals are sometimes given things like growth hormones or are
   force-fed to speed up their growth — making it even quicker and
   cheaper to produce meat.

3) Factory-farmed food is generally cheaper than free-range (see below)
   — it's a more efficient way of farming, though it isn't as ethical.

4) People are becoming more concerned that intensively reared animals
   don't live very nice lives — they're more likely to suffer from nasty
   diseases, they can't behave naturally and are killed at a young age.

Factory farmed 'broiler' chickens might
be slaughtered after only 6 weeks.

5) Some people believe that meat from factory-farmed animals
   doesn't taste as nice as meat from free-range animals.

6) Battery cages for hens were banned throughout the EU in 2012. New 'enriched cages' provide
   slightly more space and nesting areas, but some people still argue that standards could be better.

## Free-Range Animals Have More Space

Concerns for how reared animals are kept has led to an increase in people buying free-range food.

1) Free-range food (e.g. eggs) comes from animals that have more space
   to live than factory-farmed animals — they're often free to roam.

2) Free-range animals have different amounts of space depending on the
   brand you buy and aren't given hormones to speed up their growth.

3) They usually have nicer lives because of the higher standard of welfare.

4) Less food can be produced by rearing animals in free-range conditions — they use up
   energy moving around, so take longer to grow. The extra land needed also adds to the cost.
   This makes products more expensive and they might be beyond some people's budget.

5) Labels are added to foods to show they meet welfare standards. For example:

- The Red Tractor symbol on products lets consumers know that the
  producer meets standards of food safety, hygiene, animal welfare and
  environmental protection set by the Assured Food Standards scheme.
  Farm assured food can be traced back to the farms they came from.

- The RSPCA Assured symbol can be found on eggs, fish and meat — to
  get the logo, producers have to follow strict RSPCA welfare standards.
  These standards cover every part of an animal's life, including
  diet, lighting, bedding and how they're transported.

## I had this reared dream once — I was being raised by a chicken...

More ethical products are generally more expensive — you'll need to be able to explain the reasons why.
If only there were a few questions to help with that...

Q1   What is meant by free-range food?                                                          [1 mark]

Q2   Give two reasons why free-range foods are often more expensive than factory-farmed foods.   [2 marks]

# Caught Food

Fish are a super source of <u>protein</u> and really benefit the <u>human diet</u>. Sadly, some fish species are so <u>popular</u>, like <u>North Sea cod</u>, that they have almost <u>disappeared</u> from our seas due to <u>overfishing</u>.

## *There are Different Fishing Methods*

Fish can be <u>caught</u> or <u>reared</u> — the fishing method used depends on the <u>type</u> of fish and where it's <u>found</u>.

**Trawling**
- <u>Trawling</u> is a very common method of <u>fishing</u> — <u>trawlers</u> are fishing boats that catch fish using <u>nets</u>. Large trawlers may process fish on-board (<u>factory trawlers</u>).
- There are <u>different methods</u> of trawling — some <u>drag</u> a net through the <u>open sea</u>, and others along the <u>surface</u> of the <u>seabed</u> (bottom trawling).
- <u>Dredging</u> is like bottom trawling but uses a <u>metal 'basket'</u> instead of a net.

**Fish Farming**
- Large numbers of fish are <u>raised</u> in <u>tanks</u> or <u>enclosures</u> in rivers and lakes or in <u>cages</u> in the <u>sea</u>. E.g. <u>salmon</u>, <u>carp</u> and <u>trout</u>.
- As with <u>factory-farmed</u> land animals, there is <u>overcrowding</u> — the fish are more likely to suffer from <u>diseases</u>.

When the fish are <u>caught</u> they may be <u>washed</u> and <u>gutted</u> on the boats before they are brought to shore. Fish are <u>chilled</u> (packed with ice) or <u>salted</u> to prevent <u>spoilage</u> on the way to supermarkets and fishmongers.

## *Sustainable Fishing Preserves Future Fish Stocks*

There is concern over how fishing methods are <u>damaging</u> the <u>environment</u>...

Bottom trawling is <u>destructive</u>, e.g. the nets that drag across the seabed can <u>destroy corals</u>, which are a <u>habitat</u> for lots of <u>marine life</u>.

Trawlers can also catch <u>unwanted</u> animals, like <u>dolphins</u> or <u>turtles</u>, in their nets.

<u>Overfishing</u> is when <u>more fish</u> are <u>caught</u> than can be <u>replaced</u> by natural reproduction. E.g. the demand for <u>bluefin tuna</u> to make <u>sushi</u> has led to overfishing. Bluefin tuna are now endangered (at risk of going <u>extinct</u>).

...so there needs to be <u>methods</u> to <u>conserve</u> fish stocks and make fishing more <u>sustainable</u>.

**Alternative fishing methods**
E.g. <u>Longline</u> fishing uses a fishing line with <u>baited hooks</u> secured between two buoys. <u>Fewer</u> fish are caught and there is less chance of catching <u>unwanted</u> fish.

A sustainable method is one that doesn't damage the environment or use up finite resources.

**Fishing quotas**
<u>Quotas</u> set by <u>governments</u> help <u>endangered</u> species of fish. They limit the <u>amount</u> and <u>sizes</u> of fish that can be caught.

**Regulating net size**
Holes in fishing <u>nets</u> have to be a certain <u>size</u>, so that <u>smaller</u>, <u>unwanted</u> fish can escape.

Not falling for that again...

## *Sustainable fishing — we cod do batter...*

Learn the various fishing methods and how fishing can be made sustainable. Splendid! I'm off to the chippy.

Q1 Explain why bottom trawling is not considered a sustainable fishing technique. [3 marks]

# Waste Food and Packaging

Millions of tonnes of food are thrown away each year — most of which could have been avoided.
Households, food producers and retailers all contribute to food wastage.

## We Throw Away Lots of Food at Home

Households are big culprits when it comes to wasting food —
fruits, vegetables and bread are all thrown out unnecessarily.

> Oi! I was safe to eat!
> What a waste!
> How dare you!

REASONS FOR WASTING FOOD
1) Food has spoiled because:
   - It was overcooked or burnt
   - It wasn't covered or stored correctly
   - It wasn't kept at the right temperature
   - It had passed its use by date
2) Confusion over best before dates and other date marks — people wrongly think the food is no longer edible.

3) Too much food was cooked, and edible leftovers aren't frozen or reused.
4) Preparing food incorrectly — e.g. peeling vegetables too thickly.

## Producers and Retailers Waste Food Too

A lot of food is wasted during production and by shops.

REASONS FOR WASTING FOOD
1) Retailers will reject food from producers if it is damaged or spoiled during transport.
2) Imperfect food (e.g. 'ugly' looking fruit) is often rejected by retailers too — the producer can't sell it, so it gets wasted.
3) To avoid running out of stock and disappointing their customers, supermarkets stock more than they can sell. The unsold stock gets binned, including stuff that is still safe to eat, like bread.
4) Offers from supermarkets encourage people to buy more than they can use or store.
5) Larger packs of food are better value for money — but again, it's often more than people need.

## Reduce Waste and Save Money

Reducing food waste will not only help the environment, it will help people save money too.

1) Plan meals and correct portion sizes — only buy ingredients that you will use.
2) Correctly store food and pay attention to use by dates.
3) Use up the contents of your fridge before buying more food.
4) Use leftovers in meals the day after or freeze them for another time.
5) Use the whole food (e.g. bones can be used for stocks, peelings can be made into compost).
6) Donate unwanted food (cereals, pasta, beans etc.) to food banks. Some supermarkets are reducing their waste by donating unsold food.

> Food waste costs the average household around £500 a year.

## XL double bacon cheeseburger — good waist food...

Waste food and packaging (there's more about that over on the next page) can damage the environment.
Less food waste can reduce this impact and save us money, so it's a good idea to plan out your meals properly.

Q1 Simon is planning to make some spaghetti Bolognese.
Give some advice on how he could reduce food waste when preparing and cooking the meal. [3 marks]

Q2 A supermarket has a 'buy one get one free' offer on cooked ham.
Explain how this offer could have a negative impact on food waste. [2 marks]

48

# Waste Food and Packaging

Packaging is <u>pretty useful</u>, but like <u>waste food</u>, if it's <u>thrown away</u> it can damage the <u>environment</u>. Boo.

## *Packaging is Great for Manufacturers*

Manufacturers use different <u>materials</u> to <u>package food</u> — each material has certain <u>benefits</u>.

- <u>Plastic</u> (cling film, vacuum-pack bags) — <u>transparent</u>, <u>lightweight</u> and can be <u>shaped</u> to the food.
- <u>Glass</u> (milk bottles, jars) — <u>transparent</u>, <u>heat-resistant</u>, gives food a <u>long shelf life</u> and is <u>reusable</u>.
- <u>Metal</u> (tins) — <u>heat-resistant</u> and gives food a <u>long shelf life</u>.
- <u>Paper</u> (pizza boxes, egg cartons, labels) — <u>lightweight</u>, can be <u>printed on</u> and is <u>biodegradable</u>.

Choosing <u>suitable</u> packaging <u>reduces waste food</u> (and saves the <u>manufacturer money</u>) because it:

- <u>Protects</u> food from being <u>damaged</u> while it's being <u>transported</u>, <u>displayed</u> and <u>stored</u>.
- <u>Preserves</u> the food and stops <u>contamination</u> from <u>bacteria</u> or <u>pests</u>.

Packaging also shows <u>useful information</u> to help customers (see p.64).

## *Packaging can be Bad for the Environment*

<u>Excess</u> packaging is often used to make a product look more <u>appealing</u> to get a customer to buy it. But this <u>comes at a cost</u>...

1) <u>Manufacturing</u> the materials for packaging uses lots of <u>energy</u> and <u>natural resources</u> — some of which are <u>non-renewable</u> (e.g. <u>plastics</u> from <u>crude oil</u>).

2) Packaging often gets used <u>once</u>, <u>thrown away</u> and then just takes up space in Britain's already huge <u>landfill sites</u>.

3) Some packaging, like <u>plastics</u>, take a long time to <u>biodegrade</u> (decompose), and could <u>take up space</u> in a landfill site for decades.

4) Packaging adds to the <u>weight</u> of a product, so heavier materials, such as <u>metals</u> and <u>glass</u>, require more energy to <u>transport</u> them.

5) <u>Litter</u> is <u>hazardous</u> to animals too — e.g. <u>marine life</u> can get <u>entangled</u> in <u>plastics</u> or <u>eat it</u> by mistake.

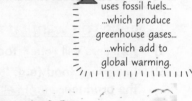
Producing energy uses fossil fuels... ...which produce greenhouse gases... ...which add to global warming.

## *You can Reduce the Environmental Impact*

1) <u>Recycling</u> uses much <u>less energy</u> than manufacturing <u>new</u> packaging...

2) ...so always <u>recycle tins</u>, <u>glass</u>, <u>card</u> and <u>paper</u> — there are recycling <u>banks</u> all around the UK and local <u>councils</u> provide <u>recycling bins / bags</u> for homes.

3) Most <u>plastics</u> (bottles, pots, tubs and trays) can be recycled too. If in doubt, the <u>labels</u> on plastic packaging will tell you which <u>materials</u> are used and <u>whether</u> you can <u>recycle</u> them.

4) Buy products with little or no packaging and <u>refuse</u> ones with <u>excess packaging</u>.

5) Choose products with <u>biodegradable packaging</u> or packaging <u>made</u> from <u>recycled materials</u>.

6) Carry food in <u>reusable shopping bags</u> to reduce the need for <u>plastic bags</u>.

Since October 2015, large shops in England have to charge 5p for a plastic bag to encourage customers to re-use them instead.

FILM PLASTIC not currently recycled

## *Suspicious packaging — don't leave bags unattended...*

So excess packaging is bad, but packaging still has an important job to do. Without it, foods would spoil and get damaged during transport, causing food waste. It's all about using the right materials... but not too much of them...

Q1 Give three ways that food packaging can have a negative impact on the environment. [3 marks]

# Food Miles and Carbon Footprint

Your food doesn't just magically appear in a supermarket — some of it's travelled thousands of miles.

## Food Comes from Different Countries

Food Miles — the distance food travels from where it's produced to the consumer.

Moon — 238,900 miles ◀▶ 1000 miles — Spanish

Cheese / Oranges

1) Some food is transported a long way to be sold, e.g. some green beans you buy in the UK have come from Kenya.

2) This is bad for the environment — planes, ships and trucks all burn scarce fossil fuels and release carbon dioxide into the atmosphere, contributing to global warming.

3) But consumers now expect food to be available all year round, not just when it's in season here. So shops and manufacturers buy food from abroad when it's out of season at home, e.g. asparagus has a very short season here. Also, some things just can't be grown here, like bananas.

4) Manufacturing costs are different in other countries, so imported food can sometimes be cheap.

## Buy Food from Local Markets to Reduce Food Miles

1) Local food is often better for the environment as it has fewer food miles.

2) Local food is often fresher and tastier because it reaches you soon after it has been harvested.

3) Buying from farmers' markets and independent greengrocers etc. supports local businesses and their produce can be cheap.

4) Check labels on foods from supermarkets too — food producers often make it a big deal on their packaging if they use ingredients from the UK.

> When planning your meals look to source local, seasonal ingredients that are in season and haven't been shipped from around the world.

So it's good for the environment, but buying locally does have downsides too:

1) Seasonal food is not available all year round, e.g. strawberries are only available in the summer, so you have a smaller selection of products.

2) Unpackaged or unpreserved foods spoil faster — you have to use them quickly.

## Carbon Footprint Measures Environmental Impact

1) Your carbon footprint measures the impact your lifestyle has on the environment.

2) It's given as the amount of greenhouse gases you directly and indirectly produce from burning fossil fuels for heat, electricity, transport etc. (usually expressed as tonnes of carbon dioxide per year).

3) Foods have a carbon footprint too — greenhouse gases are produced when growing, processing, packaging and transporting them.

The average UK person has a carbon footprint of over 10 tonnes a year.

You can reduce your carbon footprint:
- Buy food that is in season, with lower food miles and with less packaging
- Use public transport, walk or take up cycling
- Waste less energy in the home (e.g. turn TVs off standby, turn the heating down)

## From plate to mouth — 0.0001 food miles...

Brussels sprouts come into season between October and March, so they're perfect for Christmas dinners (and are the best bit of course) — buying seasonally means tastier food and cuts down on food miles from importing them.

Q1   Explain the benefits of 'pick your own' strawberries over buying from a supermarket.   [3 marks]

Q2   a) Give an example of a food product that has a high carbon footprint.   [1 mark]

    b) Explain why your chosen food product has a high carbon footprint.   [2 marks]

# Global Food Production

A great challenge we face today is to provide the world's population with a steady, sustainable supply of food. You need to understand why this is such a challenge and the effects that food poverty can have.

## Climate Change Can Affect Food Production

Processing, transporting and wasting food all lead to the production of greenhouse gases. These gases trap heat in the atmosphere and are causing our climate to change and the Earth to get hotter.

1)  Just a tiny increase in average global temperature can massively affect the production of crops:
    - Many crops will have lower yields, e.g. maize production could be reduced by millions of tonnes.
    - Pests and microorganisms can reproduce more easily and can invade new regions that were too cold for them before.

2)  Climate change can cause some extreme weather events which affect food production:

### Drought
- A drought happens in an area that has had a lack of rainfall.
- Crops struggle to grow or fail completely.
- Rivers and lakes can dry up, killing fish and other wildlife.
- Drought can cause wildfires — uncontrollable fires spread through the countryside, destroying fields and reared animals.

### Flooding
- Severe rainfall, cyclones etc. can cause major flooding.
- Floods directly damage and destroy crops.
- Soil and nutrients useful for crop growth are washed away.
- Sewage can pollute fields and spread disease in animals.
- Reared animals may drown.

Some colder countries may benefit from a warmer climate — they can grow things that they couldn't before.
E.g. more land is being used for wine grapes in southern England due to recent warm summers.

## Food Poverty is Where a Person Can't Obtain Nutritious Food

Even in a relatively rich country such as the UK, millions of people live in food poverty:

Food poverty is where a person isn't able to access or afford nutritious food.

1)  People can live in food poverty if they don't earn enough money to spend on food or have no choice but to spend it on other things, e.g. fuel bills, debts or loans.

2)  Low income households in rural areas might find it difficult to access nutritious food — households without a car or with insufficient access to public transport may have to shop in more expensive local shops, with less choice.

3)  People in food poverty may buy cheap and unhealthy foods. These foods can lead to malnutrition (due to a diet without the right balance of nutrients) and diet-related health problems such as obesity and diabetes.

4)  Families may rely on food donations from the local community (e.g. food banks), and parents may even go hungry so their children can eat.

## Today's forecast — flooding with a shortage of meatballs...

We sneaked in a bit from our Geography revision guide to see if you'd notice. Surprise! I kid... but while there is some climate change chat, remember this is a food book, so you need to link everything to food production.

Q1      Give one way that rising sea levels could affect food production.                    [1 mark]

# Global Food Production

Resources, such as food, water and energy, are necessary for a basic standard of living —
with the world's population rapidly increasing there is a greater demand for these resources.

## Food Security is Where People Have Access to Food They Need

People have food security when they have access to enough nutritious food to stay healthy and active.

1) You can talk about the food security of a person, a community, a country or the world:

A country that can produce a lot of food or is rich
enough to import the food it needs has food security.

An African community where the people can't produce enough
food or buy what they need does not have food security.

2) In 1996, the World Food Summit stated that global food security will be achieved when everyone,
at all times, has access to sufficient, safe and nutritious food for an active and healthy life.

3) The World Health Organisation describes three things we need to address to achieve global food security:

### Availability

Sufficient food needs to be produced by
countries to feed their populations and excess
food should be exported to countries that need it.

### Access

Food needs to be affordable to all, or
sufficient land and resources should be
available for people to grow their own food.

### Utilisation

Educating people on food and nutrition means people can use a
greater variety of foods, reduce food waste, retain the nutritional
value of foods and prevent illness from cross-contamination.

The Fairtrade Foundation is a
charity that supports farmers in
developing countries — a decent
price for their produce means the
farmers can be more food secure.

4) Many factors affect food security:

- Climate — some countries have climates that are unsuitable for farming (e.g. too hot or little
  rainfall). Extreme weather events, such as floods or droughts, can also affect the food supply.
- Insufficient land — people living in poverty often don't have their own land to grow food.
- Growing industrial crops — more farmland that previously grew crops for food is now being
  used to grow non-food crops, e.g. crops for biofuels (fuels from plant material).
- Wealth — wealthier people have more disposable income to spend on food, often more than
  they need. People with lower incomes may not be able to afford nutritious food.
- Rising population — the more people there are, the less food there is to go around.

## We Need to Produce More Food

With global demand for
food increasing, we need
to increase food supplies.

- Using new technologies — e.g. GM crops can be given
  pest-resistance, higher nutritional values and higher yields.
- Eating less meat — animals that are reared for their meat are fed crops
  that we grow. It's more efficient if we directly eat those crops instead.
- Reducing food waste — if less food is wasted, more is available to eat.

And we have to use sustainable techniques (e.g. when fishing — p.46) which don't damage the environment
or use up limited resources, so that enough food can continue to be grown to feed future generations.

## Don't let food security cashew stealing any nuts...

Food security is a strange term but all it means is whether someone has access to plenty of nutritious food.
Learn the factors that affect it too — you won't solve world hunger but it will help you write a great exam answer.

Q1    Sienna lives in the UK and earns a high income.
Explain whether you think Sienna does or does not have food security.                    [3 marks]

# British and International Cuisines

A <u>cuisine</u> is a style of cooking that is <u>representative</u> of a <u>particular country</u> or <u>region</u>. Different cuisines may have different <u>ingredients</u>, <u>serving styles</u> and <u>preparation techniques</u>.

## Each Part of the UK Has Its Own Dishes

1) The United Kingdom has four countries — <u>England</u>, <u>Wales</u>, <u>Scotland</u> and <u>Northern Ireland</u>.
   Great Britain just consists of England, Wales and Scotland. Not a lot of people know that.

2) Traditional cooking techniques involve <u>stewing</u>, <u>roasting</u>, <u>baking</u>, <u>grilling</u>, <u>boiling</u> and <u>frying</u>.

3) Meals are eaten <u>three</u> times a day — breakfast, lunch and dinner (or breakfast, dinner 'n' tea if yer frum up North like us).

4) Main courses usually pair <u>meat</u> or <u>fish</u> with potatoes and other vegetables and are often served with a <u>sauce</u>, e.g. roast beef with gravy.

5) Here are some traditional <u>ingredients</u> and <u>dishes</u> from across the UK:

   > <u>Meat and fish</u>: Beef, lamb, pork, haddock, eel, shellfish (e.g. crab, mussels, oysters).
   > <u>Vegetables</u>: Potato, carrot, parsnips, cabbage, leek, onion, green beans, cauliflower.
   > <u>Dairy and eggs</u>: Milk, cream, butter, cheese, chicken eggs.
   > <u>Fruit</u>: Apples, pears, strawberries, blackberries, gooseberries, rhubarb, blackcurrants.

### England

- <u>Cumberland sausage</u> — a coiled sausage flavoured with pepper and herbs.
- <u>Cottage pie</u> — beef mince, gravy and vegetables topped with grilled, mashed potato.
- <u>Cornish pasty</u> — pastry containing beef, potato, onion and swede.
- <u>Potted shrimps</u> — shrimps in melted butter.
- <u>Bread and butter pudding</u> — buttered bread soaked in milk, eggs, sugar and spices.

### Northern Ireland

- <u>Crubeens</u> — boiled pigs' feet, which are battered and fried.
- <u>Soda bread</u> — bread made with bicarbonate of soda and buttermilk instead of yeast.
- <u>Potato farl</u> (Irish potato cakes) — a savoury Irish potato pancake.
- <u>Ulster fry</u> — a fried breakfast with soda bread, potato farls, bacon, sausage, egg and tomato.

### Wales

- <u>Welsh rarebit</u> — toasted bread with a cheese sauce, often containing mustard, beer or wine.
- <u>Bara brith</u> — cake with dried fruit and spices.
- <u>Laverbread</u> — slow cooked seaweed paste.
- <u>Glamorgan sausage</u> — a vegetarian sausage made with cheese and leeks, and coated in breadcrumbs.
- <u>Welsh cakes</u> — small, round flat cakes with raisins baked on a griddle.

### Scotland

- <u>Scotch broth</u> — soup made with red meat, root vegetables, barley and dried pulses.
- <u>Neeps and tatties</u> — swede and potatoes cooked in oil and mashed.
- <u>Haggis</u> — lamb (and sometimes beef), suet, onion, oatmeal, seasoning and spices.
- <u>Shortbread</u> — a buttery and crumbly biscuit made with butter, flour and sugar.

## Modern British Cuisine Reinvents Popular Recipes

1) Modern takes on traditional recipes include <u>cottage pie</u> filled with <u>chilli con carne</u> and topped with <u>sweet potato</u>, salted-caramel <u>apple crumble</u>, and a <u>bread and butter pudding</u> made with <u>brioche</u> and <u>marmalade</u>.

2) Britain today is also a <u>multicultural</u> society that has <u>adopted</u> recipes from many other <u>cultures</u> — a very popular dish in the UK is <u>chicken tikka masala</u> (a variety of <u>curry</u>).

3) Even Britain's use of <u>common</u> 'staple foods' is changing — e.g. <u>potatoes</u> are still a <u>common ingredient</u>, but <u>rice</u> and <u>pasta</u> are becoming more <u>popular</u>.

> The <u>Eatwell Guide</u> (p.11) is the UK's most recent <u>healthy eating model</u> — it encourages people to swap <u>traditional</u> foods that are high in <u>saturated fats</u> for <u>alternatives</u>, e.g. <u>vegetable oils</u> instead of <u>butter</u> or <u>lard</u>.

# British and International Cuisines

Now we'll show you a <u>couple of examples</u> of <u>different cuisines</u>, and the <u>type of things</u> you'd need to know about them. If you've studied different cuisines, make sure you learn <u>all this and more</u> about them.

## *Traditional Japanese Meals Consist of Rice and Okazu*

1) Japanese cuisine mainly consists of <u>steamed rice</u> (gohan), combined with a number of <u>okazu</u> (dishes to eat with rice).

2) <u>Boiling</u>, <u>steaming</u> and <u>frying</u> are all popular cooking techniques.

3) <u>Rice cookers</u> and <u>woks</u> are used regularly in Japanese cooking. Bamboo steamers are used for steaming things like dumplings.

4) <u>Three</u> meals are eaten each day — in the morning, at midday, and in the early evening (the largest meal of the day).

5) Typical Japanese home-cooked dinners often have <u>one</u> course — in which multiple dishes are presented at once on separate plates or bowls.

6) Common <u>ingredients</u> in Japanese cuisine are:

> <u>Rice:</u>  Rice is eaten with nearly every meal.  It is also used to make desserts and sweets.
> <u>Noodles:</u>  Strands of dough that are stretched and cut into shapes.
> <u>Seafood:</u>  Such as salmon, mackerel, tuna, squid.  Served raw (sashimi) or grilled.
> <u>Saké/Mirin:</u>  Japanese rice-wines.  Mirin is sweeter than saké, and also has a lower alcohol content.
> <u>Pickled vegetables:</u>  Vegetables preserved in vinegar.  Served as an appetiser, side or topping.
> <u>Matcha tea:</u>  Powdered green tea.  Used in hot drinks and as flavouring in cakes, ice cream etc.

7) Common <u>dishes</u> in Japanese cuisine are:

<u>Sushi</u> — Sticky rice, often topped or rolled with raw fish (sashimi) and seaweed.

<u>Tempura</u> — Seafoods, vegetables or meat coated with batter and deep-fried.

<u>Gyoza</u> — Fried dumplings stuffed with meat or vegetables.

<u>Ramen</u> — Noodles in a soup, topped with vegetables, meat, eggs etc.

<u>Miso Soup</u> — a soup made from fermented soya beans, fungus and salt.

8) Desserts are less common in Japan than in the UK.  Sweet <u>rice cakes</u>, served with green matcha tea, are very popular.  Red bean paste is a common filling in desserts.

## *Japanese Meals are Eaten with Chopsticks*

1) <u>Chopsticks</u> are often used to pick up food, rather than using hands or cutlery.  Rice and soup bowls may be held <u>close to the mouth</u> to make them easier to eat from, but plates should be left on the table.

2) People traditionally <u>sit on floor mats</u> around low tables to eat, but many modern restaurants provide <u>Western-style tables</u> and <u>chairs</u>.

3) Soup can be <u>slurped</u> from the bowl — it shows the chef that the food is being enjoyed.

4) Raw or pickled <u>ginger</u> is used to 'cleanse the palate', e.g. with sushi.

5) Modern twists on Japanese foods include <u>fusing</u> Japanese and <u>Western</u> dishes, e.g. BBQ pulled pork gyoza, matcha tea frappés, wasabi-flavoured chocolate, and using teriyaki (a Japanese sauce) on roast meats.

> The <u>Japanese Food Pyramid</u> is Japan's most recent <u>healthy eating model</u> and is based on <u>traditional</u> Japanese foods.  It recommends 5-7 servings of <u>grains</u> (rice, noodles etc.), 5-6 servings of <u>vegetables</u>, 3-5 servings of <u>fish</u>, <u>meat</u> or <u>eggs</u>, and 2 servings of both <u>milk</u> and <u>fruits</u> to be eaten each day.

# British and International Cuisines

Here's another <u>international cuisine</u> for you.  Again, if you've been taught about two different international cuisines, make sure you know <u>this type of stuff</u> about them.

## *In Spanish Cuisine Lunch is the Largest Meal of the Day*

1)  In Spain three main meals are eaten throughout the day.  Smaller eats may occur between main meals.

2)  Typical cooking methods in Spain are stewing, charcoal grilling, plate grilling and cooking in a sauce.

3)  <u>Breakfasts</u> are <u>small</u> and <u>light</u>, and are eaten first thing in the morning. People often break for a larger snack at around 10 am.

4)  The <u>largest</u> meal of the day is <u>lunch</u> (2-4 pm), which often consists of 3 courses — a <u>starter</u>, <u>main</u>, and <u>dessert</u> and/or coffee.  <u>Dinner</u> is a <u>lighter meal</u> eaten around 9-11 pm.

5)  The Spanish lunch <u>usually</u> has three courses, but can have up to six: Appetiser, first course, fish dish, meat dish, dessert and coffee.

6)  Typical <u>ingredients</u> and <u>dishes</u> in Spanish cuisine are:

> <u>Meats</u>: Pork, chicken and seafood.
> <u>Herbs and spices</u>: Peppers, nutmeg, paprika, cumin and coriander.
> <u>Fruit and Veg</u>: Peppers, olives, garlic, tomatoes, oranges, lemons.
> <u>Other</u>: Almonds, olive oil, beans, wine (often served with meals).

<u>Churros</u>: thin strips or loops of fried dough, often dunked in hot chocolate or chocolate sauce.

<u>Serrano ham</u>: a type of cured ham.

<u>Chorizo</u>: a spicy cured pork sausage.

<u>Paella</u>: a rice dish made in a large flat pan, made with stock, seafood (such as squid, shrimp and mussels), chicken or other meats, and vegetables.  It is commonly cooked in huge portions for festivals.

<u>Patatas bravas</u>: spiced, fried potato chunks served with a spicy tomato sauce.

<u>Tapas</u>: Small savoury dishes eaten as a snack or like a buffet (where many dishes are shared between a group of people).  Examples include: king prawns in garlic and chilli, patatas bravas (see above), chorizo (see above), grilled fish, fried squid, filled tortillas, Spanish omelette.

7)  Traditional Spanish recipes have been <u>modernised</u> in many ways, such as using quinoa or noodles in paella, and flavoured churros.  Chorizo is often used in <u>non-Spanish</u> dishes like pasta or omelettes.

The <u>NAOS Food Pyramid</u> is Spain's most recent <u>healthy eating model</u> which promotes a <u>Mediterranean</u> diet. It is divided into <u>three</u> sections to show the types of food that should be eaten <u>daily</u> (wholegrain cereals, fruits, vegetables), <u>weekly</u> (fish, red meat, eggs) and <u>occasionally</u> (sweets and snacks).

## *This is REALLY making me want a holiday to Tokyo or Barcelona...*

You'll need to be able to write about all the stuff on these pages.  If you've already learned about two other types of international cuisine, make sure that you can rhyme off the type of facts shown on these pages.

Q1   Describe three traditional British dishes, stating the country that they come from.   [3 marks]

Q2   Choose an international cuisine and: a) list four ingredients commonly used in it.   [2 marks]

b) describe three traditional dishes associated with it.   [3 marks]

# Primary Food Processing

All food goes through stages of processing before it reaches our plate. It's important so that food is safe to eat, is easier to transport, doesn't spoil as quickly and looks nice for the consumer.

## Primary Processing *Changes Raw Foods*

Primary processing prepares raw foods (straight from being picked, harvested or slaughtered) so they're ready either to be eaten or cooked immediately or used as ingredients to make other food products.

Primary stages of processing include transporting food from its point of origin (the place where it's grown or reared), as well as cleaning, sorting, milling etc.

### Fruit / Vegetables

*   Pits (stones) are removed from fruit, e.g. peaches and cherries.
*   Fruits are squeezed for fruit juices or dried, e.g. grapes are sun-dried to make raisins.
*   Fruits and vegetables are washed with water to remove dirt, insects and chemical sprays.
*   Fruits and vegetables are sorted into different sizes and shapes.
*   Fruits and seeds are crushed or pressed to extract oils, e.g. olive oil.

> Washing might be the first primary stage of processing, e.g. when preparing a bag of fruit.

### Meat / Poultry

*   Some meats (e.g. beef) are hung and dried to make them more tender and improve flavour.
*   Feathers and internal organs of poultry are removed.
*   The wings and legs of poultry are tied (trussed) so it cooks evenly.
*   Meat is chopped, sliced or cut.

### Wheat

Flour is made by milling wheat grains:

1) Wheat grains (seeds) are harvested and then cleaned to remove any stones, dust etc.

2) The grains are stored in dry conditions to prevent moulds from growing on them.

3) The grains are put into a hopper and are crushed between rollers that crack open the grain.

4) Different types of flour can be made by sieving and removing parts of the grain (wholemeal flour uses all of the grain and white flour only uses about 70% of the grain).

A wheat grain
Bran (mostly fibre)
Endosperm (mostly starch)
Germ (vitamins, protein and fat)

### Milk

Raw milk goes through a primary stage of processing (heat treatment) to destroy any pathogenic bacteria and make it safe to drink. Examples of heat treatments include:

*   Pasteurisation — Milk is heated quickly to 72 °C for 15 seconds and then rapidly cooled.
*   Ultra Heat Treatment (UHT) — Milk is heated to at least 135 °C for 1-4 seconds and packed in a sterile container — the milk can be stored in a cool, dry place (see p.39) for several months.

## Processing *Affects* Sensory *and* Nutritional *Properties*

Processing a food can change how it looks and tastes, as well as its nutritional content. For example:

*   Fish and meat products might be salt-cured (preserved with salt) — this gives them a salty taste.
*   There's lots of fibre in the skin of a potato — peeling the skin removes this important source of fibre.
*   High temperatures can destroy vitamins, e.g. when using UHT for milk or boiling fruit (next page) for jam.

# Secondary Food Processing

## Secondary Processing Uses Primary Processed Foods

After <u>primary processing</u> comes, surprisingly, <u>secondary processing</u>. Primary processed foods are turned into <u>other food products</u> by <u>altering</u> them in some way or <u>combining</u> them with other ingredients.

## Flour can be Turned into Pasta and Bread

Flour goes through <u>secondary</u> stages of processing to turn it into <u>pasta</u> and <u>bread</u>:

**Pasta**
1) Flour is <u>mixed</u> with <u>water</u> or <u>eggs</u> to make a dough.
2) The dough is <u>shaped</u> by forcing it through a <u>metal die</u> and then <u>folded</u> / <u>twisted</u> etc.
3) <u>Colourings</u> may be added to dye the pasta (e.g. <u>spinach</u> for a <u>green</u> pasta).
4) The pasta may be <u>dried</u> or eaten <u>fresh</u>.

Pasta usually uses <u>semolina</u> flour — it comes from milling a type of wheat known as <u>durum</u> wheat.

**Bread**
1) Flour is <u>mixed</u> with <u>water</u> and <u>yeast</u> to make a dough.
2) The dough is <u>kneaded</u> to 'work' the gluten (see p.29).
3) The dough is <u>proved</u> to let the yeast <u>ferment</u> (see p.33).
4) The dough is <u>baked</u> in an oven.

## Fruit can be Turned into Jam and Jellies

→ E.g. filtering, pasteurising and packaging.

Fruit goes through <u>secondary</u> stages of processing to turn it into <u>juice</u>, <u>jam</u> (a <u>fruit preserve</u>) and <u>jelly</u>:

**Jam**
1) <u>Crushed fruit</u> is mixed with <u>sugar</u>.
2) The mixture is <u>boiled</u> (to at least <u>105 °C</u>) and left to cool.
3) <u>Pectin</u> (a gelling substance in the fruit) <u>thickens</u> the jam as it cools.
4) Jam is <u>poured</u> into glass jars which are <u>sealed</u> to extend its shelf life.

**Jelly**
1) <u>Fruit juice</u> is mixed with <u>sugar</u> and heated.
2) <u>Gelatine</u> (a gelling substance from animal products) is soaked in <u>cold water</u> to <u>soften</u> and then added to the hot mixture.
3) The mixture is <u>sieved</u> to remove <u>lumps</u> or <u>pips</u>.
4) The mixture is <u>refrigerated</u> — the gelatine <u>thickens</u> and <u>sets</u> the jelly.

Pectin must be added if low-pectin fruits are used, e.g. raspberries, so that the jam sets properly.

## Milk can be Turned into Cheese

Milk is also processed to make yoghurt — see p.34.

**①** For most types of cheese, raw milk is <u>pasteurised</u> to kill off any <u>pathogenic bacteria</u>.

Bacteria          Rennet
**②** 'Friendly' bacteria <u>sour</u> and <u>thicken</u> the milk, and <u>rennet</u> from calf stomachs is added. A vegetarian alternative to rennet can be used.

Curds          Whey
**③** Rennet causes the milk to <u>coagulate</u> into solid <u>cheese curds</u>. The liquid remaining is called <u>whey</u>.

**④** The whey is removed by either <u>draining</u>, <u>cutting</u>, <u>cooking</u>, <u>salting</u> or <u>stacking</u> curds on top of each other (<u>cheddaring</u>).

**⑤** The curds are <u>pressed</u> to form <u>blocks</u> of cheese and placed in temperature-controlled storage to 'mature' and develop <u>taste</u> and <u>texture</u>.

**⑥** <u>Bacteria</u> or <u>moulds</u> may be added to change the <u>flavour</u> of the cheese (see p.34).

## No whey — he's fallen at the final curdle...

Two cheese puns in one... I do like to treat you sometimes. These pages describe the stages of processing you'll need to know — check the Internet too, as there are lots of videos that show these processes in action.

Q1    Suggest two primary processes that a walnut might undergo.    [2 marks]

Q2    Explain why bread is an example of a secondary processed food.    [3 marks]

# Food Fortification and Modification

Today's <u>technology</u> allows manufacturers to add <u>vitamins</u> and <u>minerals</u> to <u>food products</u> — some people claim that this is an <u>effective method</u> of improving our health and <u>preventing deficiencies</u> in the diet.

## *Fortification Adds Nutrients to a Food*

1) <u>Fortification</u> is where <u>nutrients</u> are <u>added</u> to a food.

2) It improves the <u>nutritional value</u> of foods.

3) Fortification is done for <u>different reasons</u> — sometimes it's to <u>replace nutrients</u> lost during processing, or to <u>add extra nutrients</u> to make a food more <u>nutrient-rich</u>.

4) Here are some <u>common</u> foods that are fortified:

*Take a look through p.1–10 to see why we need nutrients in our diet.*

### White Flour

- <u>Iron</u>, <u>thiamin</u> **(B1)**, <u>niacin</u> **(B3)** and <u>calcium</u> are <u>lost</u> during the production of <u>white flour</u> **(p.55)**.
- By <u>law</u>, these nutrients have to be <u>added back in</u> — they aren't added to <u>wholemeal flour</u> because the nutrients are <u>naturally present</u>.

### Breakfast Cereals

- Cereals can be fortified with <u>iron</u>, <u>thiamin</u> and <u>folic acid</u>.
- Cereal is eaten by lots of people — if <u>manufacturers choose</u> to fortify their products it <u>helps</u> the population get the <u>recommended amounts</u> of these nutrients.

### Butter Alternatives

- Many people use <u>butter alternatives</u>, e.g. <u>margarine</u> and <u>low-fat spreads</u>.
- <u>Butter</u> naturally contains <u>vitamins A and D</u> — by <u>fortifying</u> butter alternatives, consumers don't miss out on these important vitamins.
- Margarine and low-fat spreads are usually fortified on a <u>voluntary basis</u> by manufacturers.

### Cholesterol Lowering Spreads

- Some <u>vegetable fat spreads</u> have added plant <u>sterols</u>.
- These substances help <u>reduce cholesterol</u> for people with <u>high</u> cholesterol only — they don't benefit people with normal cholesterol levels.

5) <u>Manufacturers</u> may fortify processed foods as a '<u>marketing tool</u>' — it can give the <u>impression</u> that their products are <u>healthy</u>.

6) You should be careful eating <u>excessive</u> amounts of fortified foods — you may get <u>too much</u> of some vitamins or minerals in your diet.

<u>Multivitamin supplements</u> are <u>hugely popular</u>:

- Multivitamin supplements are full of <u>vitamins</u> and <u>minerals</u> your body needs — they're <u>handy</u> if you <u>don't get enough</u> from your <u>normal diet</u> but should <u>never</u> replace a healthy, balanced diet.
- They are <u>more useful</u> for <u>certain people</u>, e.g. <u>elderly adults</u> (see p.13) and <u>pregnant women</u>.
- However, it's <u>debatable</u> whether they make <u>any difference</u> for <u>most people</u> and taking too many could be <u>harmful</u> to your health.

## *Cramming doughnuts with vitamins? Modify can help it...*

"But CGP, why can't we just add vitamins to junk food to make it healthy?" Unfortunately, this isn't going to make junk food magically any healthier — remember, these foods are still packed with sugar, salt and fats. Sad face.

Q1    Explain why a milk substitute like soya milk might be fortified.    [2 marks]

Q2    Gerardo's diet consists of many fortified foods.
       Explain why Gerardo should be careful taking vitamin supplements with his normal diet.    [2 marks]

# Food Fortification and Modification

There are other ways of <u>modifying</u> food products so they're nicer than ever — mmm, read on...

## Additives *Change the Properties of Food*

1) An <u>additive</u> is something that's <u>added</u> to food to <u>improve its properties</u>.
2) Some additives occur <u>naturally</u> and some are made <u>artificially</u>.

<u>Preservatives</u> are additives that <u>prevent bacteria from growing</u> — so the <u>food lasts longer</u>.
- Natural preservatives include <u>vinegar</u>, <u>lemon juice</u>, <u>salt</u> and <u>sugar</u>.
- Artificial preservatives include things like <u>nitrates</u> and <u>sulphites</u>.

> Important in food safety — see p.36.

<u>Colourings</u> make food look more <u>attractive</u> and more <u>appealing</u> to eat. They can be used to <u>add colour</u> to something that is <u>colourless</u>, or to <u>return</u> food to its natural colour if it's <u>lost</u> during <u>processing</u>.
- <u>Caramel</u> is a <u>natural</u> food colouring — it can make products darkish brown, e.g. <u>cola</u>.
- <u>Tartrazine</u> is an <u>artificial</u> food colouring — it's used to make products a <u>yellow</u> colour, e.g. <u>custard powder</u>, <u>syrups</u>, <u>sweets</u>.

> Tartrazine combined with a blue colouring produces the green used for mushy peas.

<u>Flavourings</u> <u>add</u> new flavours and <u>flavour enhancers</u> <u>improve</u> the existing flavour of a product.
- <u>Natural</u> flavourings include <u>herbs</u> and <u>spices</u>, e.g. <u>basil</u>, <u>chillies</u> and <u>vanilla</u>.
- <u>Artificial sweeteners</u>, e.g. <u>aspartame</u>, are used as <u>substitutes</u> for <u>sugar</u>.
- <u>Monosodium glutamate</u> (MSG) is an example of a <u>flavour enhancer</u> — it boosts the existing flavour of a product and gives it a <u>savoury taste</u>.

> <u>Natural</u> sugar alternatives like xylitol and stevia are becoming more popular now, e.g. in soft drinks.

<u>Emulsifiers and stabilisers</u> help <u>preserve</u> the <u>shape</u> and <u>texture</u> of food products (see p.32).

<u>Emulsifiers</u> help <u>mix together</u> ingredients that <u>don't usually mix</u>, e.g. <u>oily</u> and <u>watery liquids</u>.
<u>Stabilisers</u> stop mixed ingredients from <u>separating</u>.
- <u>Lecithin</u> is a <u>natural emulsifier</u> found in <u>egg yolks</u> and <u>soya beans</u>.
- <u>Pectin</u> is a <u>natural stabiliser</u> found in <u>berries</u>, <u>apples</u> and many other <u>fruits</u>.

## Additives *Have Disadvantages Too*

1) Additives, such as <u>sulphites</u> (found in <u>bacon</u> or <u>salami</u>), can cause <u>allergic reactions</u> and worsen <u>asthma</u>.
2) Some <u>natural</u> additives, like <u>sugar</u> and <u>salt</u>, are <u>bad</u> for our <u>health</u> in <u>large amounts</u>.
3) They can disguise <u>poor quality ingredients</u>, e.g. processed meat products may not contain much meat but can be made to <u>taste good</u> by using additives.
4) Additives must pass a <u>safety test</u> before they can be used in food — when an additive passes it gets an <u>E number</u> and can be used throughout the <u>European Union</u>, e.g. caramel colouring is E150a...
5) ...but there are concerns about possible <u>long-term health effects</u>. Some research <u>suggests</u> that at least six colourings: <u>sunset yellow</u> (E110), <u>quinoline yellow</u> (E104), <u>carmoisine</u> (E122), <u>allura red</u> (E129), <u>tartrazine</u> (E102), and <u>ponceau 4R</u> (E124) cause <u>hyperactive behaviour</u> in children.

---

### This sentence needs an emulsifier...

Food additives are really handy and lots of processed foods are chockablock with them, but there is concern about the long term health effects that some additives may cause.

Q1     Explain why a manufacturer might add colourings to sweets.            [1 mark]

Q2     Give three reasons why a consumer might choose a frozen lasagne with <u>no</u> artificial additives.     [3 marks]

# Revision Questions for Section Four

Phew, section 4 was a looooong one but you've finally reached one of these revision question pages again...

- Try these questions and tick off each one when you get it right.
- When you've done all the questions for a topic and are completely happy with it, tick off the topic.

## Grown, Reared and Caught Food (p.43-46) ☑

1) What is meant by 'intensive farming'?
2) Give one disadvantage of using pesticides.
3) Describe an alternative to using a pesticide as a method of controlling pests.
4) What is meant by 'organic farming'?
5) What is a 'genetically modified' food?
6) List five advantages and three disadvantages of growing GM foods.
7) Explain the difference between a 'factory-farmed' and a 'free-range' animal.
8) What does the 'Red Tractor' symbol mean on food packaging?
9) Describe two different fishing methods.
10) Explain how unsustainable fishing can damage the environment.

## Waste Food and Packaging (p.47-48) ☑

11) List lots of ways that food is wasted:  a) in the home     b) by producers and retailers.
12) Explain why using excessive packaging is bad for the environment.
13) List three ways that we can help to reduce food packaging waste.

## Food Miles, Carbon Footprint and Global Food Production (p.49-51) ☑

14) What is meant by 'food miles'?
15) Give a reason why bananas are imported to the UK.
16) List four advantages and two disadvantages of only buying local food.
17) Name three things that increase your carbon footprint.
18) What is meant by food poverty?
19) What is meant by food security?  Describe five factors that affect global food security.

## British and International Cuisines (p.52-54) ☑

20) For British, Japanese and Spanish cuisine (or two international cuisines of your choice):
    a) Describe the equipment / cooking methods used.
    b) Describe the eating patterns, e.g. when and how food is eaten.
    c) Describe four traditional foods or dishes.
    d) Describe two modern twists on traditional dishes.

## Food Processing, Fortification and Modification (p.55-58) ☑

21) Give one example of a primary stage of processing that might be used for each food below:
    a) cherry     b) potato     c) chicken
22) Give one example of how the sensory properties of a food are affected by food processing.
23) Explain how these food products are made:  a) pasta     b) jam     c) jelly     d) cheese
24) What is meant by food 'fortification'?  List four food products that are commonly fortified.
25) Give an example for each type of additive and say what it does:
    a) preservatives     b) colourings     c) flavour enhancers     d) emulsifiers     e) stabilisers
26) List four disadvantages of using food additives.

# Influences on Food Choice

There are loads of different things that affect your <u>food choices</u>.
Fortunately, this section will break them down into small, digestible, chocolate-coated chunks...

## *Many Factors Influence What People Choose to Eat*

You need to learn these <u>10 factors</u> which influence people's food choices.

### Physical Activity Level (PAL)

- Different people have different physical activity levels (PALs, see p.16). People with higher PALs need <u>more calories</u>.
- A person who has an <u>active</u> lifestyle (e.g. someone who walks 3 or more miles a day) will need to consume around 20% more calories per day than someone with a <u>sedentary</u> (inactive) lifestyle.
- Sportsmen/sportswomen may choose food to help <u>improve</u> their <u>performance</u>, e.g. <u>high protein</u> foods to help build <u>muscle</u>, or high carb foods to help with <u>endurance</u>.

### Healthy Eating

- People trying to eat <u>healthily</u> will choose foods based on their <u>nutritional</u> value, e.g. foods <u>low</u> in <u>sugar</u> and <u>fat</u>, and high in <u>vitamins</u> and other nutrients.
- People with <u>allergies</u> or <u>intolerances</u> will need to avoid certain foods.

Obligatory healthy veg pic

### Cost of Food

- People choose food based on its <u>price</u>. Generally, they'll go for the <u>cheaper</u> option, unless they think it's worth paying more for <u>better quality</u> (see below).
- People will go for foods on <u>special offer</u> — everyone likes a bargain (see p.66).
- Supermarkets often show a <u>price per gram</u> to help people compare different products. Some people will buy food in <u>bulk</u> to get a lower price per gram.
- It can be <u>cheaper per portion</u> to <u>make</u> your own food than buy ready meals, but it'll usually cost more to buy the ingredients all at once than buy a single ready meal.

*You should be able to cost your recipes. See p.19 for more information.*

### Income

- People on <u>high</u> incomes are more likely to buy <u>expensive</u> items, because a high price means (or at least suggests) it's of a higher <u>quality</u>.
- People on <u>low incomes</u> are more likely to go for the <u>cheaper</u> food option. Fresh meat, fruit and vegetables can be <u>pricey</u>, so it's more likely they'll opt for <u>cheaper</u>, <u>processed</u> foods (often high in fat and salt).
- In general, people on <u>lower</u> incomes tend to have <u>poorer</u> diets than high income groups.

### Culinary Skills

- Some people are <u>great</u> cooks, some are more "<u>beans on toast</u>". Many people just lack the <u>confidence</u> to cook.
- People may not try <u>difficult-looking</u> recipes in case it all goes wrong or they just don't enjoy it. They may not want to risk <u>wasting</u> their money on ingredients, especially if a <u>ready-made</u> alternative is available.

Caution: Overconfidence may lead to loss of digits.

# Influences on Food Choice

What, more? Learn as many of these <u>influences</u> as possible, and the <u>reasons</u> behind them.

## Lifestyle

- People who are feeling <u>stressed</u> or <u>bored</u> are more likely to go for <u>comfort food</u> (generally <u>high</u> in <u>fat</u> or <u>sugar</u>).
- People leading <u>busy</u> lives, e.g. long working hours or time-consuming hobbies, can <u>struggle</u> to find time to make a proper meal. This can make it tempting to just grab unhealthy food 'on the go'.
- People have different eating <u>patterns</u> — some have proper meals at set times of day, others tend to 'graze' throughout the day.
- Some people have <u>bad habits</u> like eating very late just before bed (not good for digestion) or regularly <u>skipping breakfast</u> (probably the worst sin of all).

With Rita's dedication to weaving, she had no time to prepare meals.

## Seasonality

- Certain UK grown foods are only available at <u>certain times</u> of year. For example, UK grown courgettes are available between June and September (see p.49).
- People worried about the environmental impact of <u>food miles</u> (see p.49) may buy <u>local foods</u> that are in season and <u>avoid</u> imports from around the world.

## Availability

- People are more likely to buy and eat foods which are readily <u>available</u>. E.g. people in <u>rural</u> areas may have to shop at a <u>small local store</u> with <u>limited</u> food options.
- However, with <u>online shopping</u> on the rise, more and more people in rural areas are able to order online and have the supermarkets <u>deliver to them</u>. Handy.

## Special Occasions

- Special occasions are often <u>celebrated</u> with a <u>large meal</u>. E.g. Fattening meals such as <u>turkey roast</u> and <u>suet pudding</u> are served at Christmas time in the UK, but they are far less common at other times of year.

## Enjoyment

- Unsurprisingly, people tend to choose the food that they <u>enjoy</u>.
- You might think that it's all about <u>flavour</u>, but <u>smell</u>, <u>appearance</u> and <u>texture</u> all affect a food's <u>palatability</u> (how appealing it is).
- One downside of eating what you enjoy is it's often not very healthy. Humans are generally drawn towards <u>sweet</u> or <u>fatty</u> foods.
- People generally aren't drawn towards <u>bitter</u> foods, although some bitter foods are hugely popular once you get the 'taste' for them, e.g. coffee, dark chocolate, beer...

## *When I click my fingers you'll crave mashed potato...*

Some of these influences may seem obvious, some may surprise you. Regardless, learn them all then try this.

Q1    Explain how a low income can affect food choice and diet.    [2 marks]

Q2    Explain how working long shifts and high levels of stress can lead to weight gain.    [3 marks]

# Cultural, Religious and Moral Food Choices

Many <u>cultures</u> and <u>religions</u> have their own <u>customs</u> around what they <u>do</u> and <u>don't</u> eat. In some there are <u>strict rules</u>, in others it's more <u>guidance</u>.

## Different Religions *Have Different* Views *on Food*

Many religions have specific dietary laws that should be followed.

**Hinduism**
1) Many Hindus are <u>vegetarian</u>, but some tend to avoid certain <u>vegetables</u> that are considered harmful such as <u>garlic</u>, <u>onion</u> and <u>mushrooms</u>.
2) The Hindus that eat meat require that it be slaughtered using a quick, painless method called <u>Jhatka</u>. In Hinduism <u>cows</u> are considered sacred, so Hindus are <u>not</u> allowed to eat <u>beef</u>.

**Islam**
1) The Qur'an states that meats eaten by muslims must be <u>halal</u> — where the lawful animal is slaughtered in a specific way whilst being blessed.
2) Muslims <u>cannot</u> eat <u>pork</u>, nor any product made from pigs, such as <u>gelatine</u>. Muslims are also not allowed to drink <u>alcohol</u>.
3) During <u>Ramadan</u> (the ninth month of the lunar calendar), Muslims <u>fast</u> between sunrise and sunset.

In the <u>lunar calendar</u>, each month has 29-30 days and Ramadan falls at a different time each year.

Fasting is when no food is eaten for a period of time.

**Judaism**
1) Jewish dietary laws (kashrut) state that their food must be <u>kosher</u> (meaning <u>fit for consumption</u>).
2) Kosher animals are ones which have split hooves <u>and</u> chew cud (such as cows and deer), plus fish that have <u>fins</u> and <u>scales</u> (so <u>no shellfish</u>). These animals must be slaughtered using quick, painless methods which allow the blood to drain afterwards, as blood is considered non-kosher.
3) Jews are <u>not</u> allowed to eat <u>pig</u>, <u>rabbit</u>, <u>hare</u>, <u>camel</u> and many other animals.
4) Dairy and meats must <u>not</u> be cooked together or eaten together as a mixture.

**Christianity**
1) There are no strict rules about foods in Christianity.
2) During <u>Lent</u>, Christians often choose to <u>give up</u> certain foods or drinks.
3) During various Christian celebrations, special foods are eaten. E.g. <u>Hot cross buns</u> on Good Friday (to represent the crucifixion of Jesus), and <u>pancakes</u> to mark the start of Lent (by using up excess ingredients).

**Sikhism**
1) Baptised Sikhs are <u>prohibited</u> from eating meat which is ritually slaughtered (such as halal or kosher meat)
2) Many Sikhs are <u>vegetarians</u>.
3) Sikhism teaches that its followers should only eat what they <u>need</u> to, and should avoid <u>overindulging</u>.

For more on planning food for groups, see p.19-21.

**Buddhism**
1) Buddhists believe that all living beings are <u>sacred</u>, so the majority of Buddhists are <u>vegetarian</u> or <u>vegan</u> (although there are no strict rules on this).
2) Most Buddhists avoid <u>alcohol</u>, as they believe it wrongly alters your view of the world around you.
3) Some Buddhists choose to <u>fast</u> from <u>noon</u> until sunrise the following day.

**Rastafarianism**
1) Eating <u>pork</u> is forbidden in Rastafarianism.
2) Many Rastafarians stick to an <u>I-tal</u> (<u>clean and natural</u>) diet, meaning the diets are mainly made up of fresh <u>vegetables</u>. Some eat fish, but the fish must be <u>less</u> than 30 cm long.
3) Many Rastafarians <u>do not</u> drink <u>alcohol</u> but <u>will</u> drink things made from natural, grown products, such as <u>herbal tea</u> or <u>fruit juice</u>.

Section Five — Factors Affecting Food Choice

# Cultural, Religious and Moral Food Choices

There's more to food choice than just being picky. Some people choose their food based on personal preferences, whereas others must choose carefully to avoid getting very ill.

## Personal Choices can be Based on Moral or Ethical Concerns

Personal choice is often based on a person's idea of what is right and wrong (their 'moral' and 'ethical' concerns). Here are some of these concerns:

### Animal Welfare

Animal welfare is a concern for many people. People may choose to eat foods where they know the animals have been treated ethically, such as free-range products (p.45), or they may avoid meat altogether, e.g. vegetarians, vegans (p.20).

### Working Conditions

- Fairtrade products, e.g. bananas, are popular with customers who want to make sure the farmers in developing countries get a fair price for their produce.
- Fairtrade products are often slightly more expensive to buy than non-Fairtrade items.

### Environmental Impact

- People may prefer to buy British or local produce, or foods that are in season, in order to support the local economy and to reduce food miles (see p.49).
- Some fish products say whether the fish were caught using sustainable fishing methods, to avoid damaging the ecosystem and stop fish from going extinct (see p.46).

### Eating Naturally

- Some people prefer to eat organic foods (p.43) — ones that have been produced without the use of synthetic chemicals. Organic foods are grown using natural fertilisers and natural pest control.
- People may avoid buying genetically modified foods, over concerns about unwanted effects on the consumer and environment (p.44).

## People with Intolerances or Allergies Must Avoid Certain Foods

1) Some people are intolerant to particular ingredients in food (p.20). Eating the food can lead to illness, and cause bloating, vomiting, pains etc.

2) Common intolerances are lactose (found in dairy products) and gluten (found in wheat, barley, oats and rye).

3) Food allergies may cause serious illness and can be fatal (p.20). Something that causes an allergic reaction is called an allergen.

4) The most common allergens are nuts, eggs, dairy, wheat, fish and shellfish.

5) It's important that food is properly labelled so that people with allergies know what they can safely eat.

## X-Melon: Acropalypse, coming soon to a field near you...

Go back through the page and think up some moral/ethical arguments for the influences above, then try these.

Q1   Explain how people may choose their food to support trade in developing countries.   [2 marks]

Q2   What dietary laws must Muslims follow?   [2 marks]

# Food Labelling

<u>Food labels</u> can help people make <u>informed choices</u> about what they eat. There are <u>tonnes</u> of <u>rules</u> about what must appear on food labels and unfortunately you'll have to <u>learn them</u>.

## *Food Label Info is Controlled by Different Regulations*

1) Countries in the <u>European Union</u> (EU) must follow the rules in the <u>Food Information for Consumers</u> regulations (FIC), updated in 2014.

2) The UK currently follows the regulations set out by the EU:
   - Food labels must not be <u>misleading</u>, e.g. making claims that the food can cure illness.
   - They must be <u>clear</u> and easy to read.
   - Common <u>allergens</u> must be <u>emphasised</u> (e.g. highlighted, bolded) in the <u>ingredients</u>.

3) From December 2016 it is <u>compulsory</u> for nutritional information to appear on food labels (next page).

4) In the UK, the <u>Food Standards Agency (FSA)</u> is responsible for making sure that food manufacturers and businesses are following the regulations (correctly labelling foods, using safe, hygienic practices, etc.).

## *Labels Must Tell You Certain Information by Law*

EU laws say that the labels on pre-packed food <u>have</u> to tell you all this stuff:

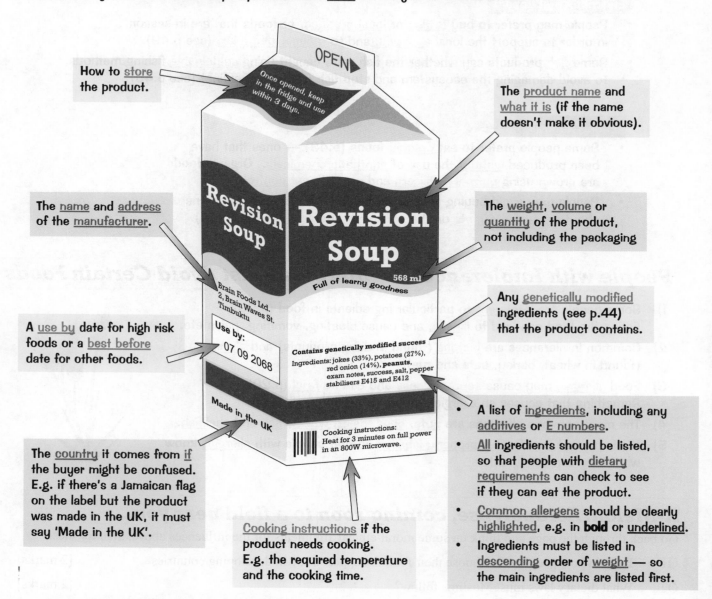

How to <u>store</u> the product.

Once opened, keep in the fridge and use within 3 days.

The <u>product name</u> and <u>what it is</u> (if the name doesn't make it obvious).

The <u>name</u> and <u>address</u> of the <u>manufacturer</u>.

The <u>weight</u>, <u>volume</u> or <u>quantity</u> of the product, not including the packaging

**Revision Soup**

Full of learny goodness

568 ml

Brain Foods Ltd.
2, Brain Waves St.
Timbuktu

Use by:
07 09 2068

A <u>use by</u> date for high risk foods or a <u>best before</u> date for other foods.

Any <u>genetically modified</u> ingredients (see p.44) that the product contains.

**Contains genetically modified success**
Ingredients: jokes (33%), potatoes (27%), red onion (14%), **peanuts**, exam notes, success, salt, pepper stabilisers E415 and E412

Made in the UK

Cooking instructions:
Heat for 3 minutes on full power in an 800W microwave.

The <u>country</u> it comes from <u>if</u> the buyer might be confused. E.g. if there's a Jamaican flag on the label but the product was made in the UK, it must say 'Made in the UK'.

<u>Cooking instructions</u> if the product needs cooking. E.g. the required temperature and the cooking time.

- A list of <u>ingredients</u>, including any <u>additives</u> or <u>E numbers</u>.
- <u>All</u> ingredients should be listed, so that people with <u>dietary requirements</u> can check to see if they can eat the product.
- <u>Common allergens</u> should be clearly <u>highlighted</u>, e.g. in **bold** or <u>underlined</u>.
- Ingredients must be listed in <u>descending</u> order of <u>weight</u> — so the main ingredients are listed first.

# Food Labelling

Packaged food products should display certain <u>nutritional information</u>. This page will teach you all about it.

## Nutritional Information *must be Shown on Food Products*

1) Since <u>December 2016</u>, manufacturers have had to include specific <u>nutritional information</u> on their packaging, although many have done this for years already.

2) Nutritional information should be shown in a <u>table</u> like this:

*Energy is always given as kilojoules (kJ) and kilocalories, and the rest are given as grams.*

| NUTRITIONAL INFORMATION | | |
|---|---|---|
| | per 100 g | per 55 g serving |
| Energy | 2180 kJ/525 kcal | 1199 kJ/289 kcal |
| Fat | 33.0 g | 18.2 g |
| of which saturates | 15.0 g | 8.3 g |
| Carbohydrate | 50.0 g | 27.5 g |
| of which sugars | 2.0 g | 1.1 g |
| Protein | 6.5 g | 3.6 g |
| Salt | 0.7 g | 0.4 g |

*Each nutrient must be given per <u>100 g</u> of the food.*

3) Other nutrient details <u>may</u> be listed, such as the amount of <u>fibre</u>, <u>vitamins</u> and <u>minerals</u>. This is not necessary, so it's up to the manufacturer to decide.

## Labels *Have Non-Compulsory Information on Them Too*

Lots of other information that <u>doesn't have to be there</u> is often found on food packaging...

Product labels often make claims about the product in order to make the product look more <u>attractive</u> and <u>improve sales</u> (see next page). This is stuff like:

- <u>High in protein</u>
- <u>Low in fat</u>
- <u>Free</u> from <u>artificial colours</u> and <u>preservatives</u>

*Food labelling rules are very strict and claims about health benefits must be truthful and accurate.*

<u>Traffic-light labelling</u> on a product shows how <u>healthy</u> it is <u>at a glance</u>. They use Reference Intake values to show whether a product has <u>high</u>, <u>medium</u> or <u>low</u> amounts of fat, salt and sugar. For example, a <u>pizza</u> might be red for fat and yellow for salt and sugar.

per 54 g serving
Fat 2.4 g — 2% | Salt 0.2 g — 4% | Sugars 9.1 g — 10%
*% reference intake of an average adult*

Products often state whether they are suitable for certain groups, e.g. <u>vegetarians</u>, <u>vegans</u>, <u>muslims</u> (halal) and <u>coeliacs</u> (gluten-free) to make it <u>easier</u> for them to pick out the <u>correct</u> products.

Labels may say where the food / ingredients are <u>from</u> and where they were <u>packaged</u> or <u>processed</u>, e.g. 'Country of origin: Spain', 'Packaged in the UK'.

Labels may include <u>serving suggestions</u>, e.g. 'Try it with custard and a dollop of ketchup.'

## *CAUTION: Book may be hot whilst burning...*

Make sure you know which things must legally be on the label, then give these questions a try. Such fun.

Q1 Calum is designing a label for his food product. So far, he's listed the ingredients.

    a) Why is it important that all of the ingredients are listed? [2 marks]

    b) State four pieces of information, other than the ingredients, that the label must include. [2 marks]

Q2 Explain two examples of non-compulsory information often given on food products. [2 marks]

# Influences of Marketing

You find <u>food adverts</u> everywhere — from <u>TV ads</u> and <u>social media</u> to <u>magazines</u> and <u>posters</u>. There's more to marketing than just ads though. This page covers some of the <u>clever tricks</u> used to pull in customers.

## *Special Offers — the Oldest Trick in the Trolley*

1) <u>Special offers</u> on food are a common sight in supermarkets.

2) Offers are used to <u>convince</u> customers to buy a product (or a quantity of it) that they wouldn't normally buy, by making it feel like they're getting a <u>bargain</u>.

> <u>Examples of special offers are:</u>
> - 'Buy one get one free' (BOGOF) or 'buy two, get the third free'
> - Reduced price (e.g. '30% off', or 'save £1.50')
> - Meal deals (e.g. main meal, dessert and a drink for £10)

3) <u>Loyalty card schemes</u> (where you get points for your shopping) allow supermarkets to record data about what you're buying, which they can use to send you offers <u>matched</u> to your <u>buying habits</u>.

4) <u>Point of sale marketing</u> is used near the till — <u>carefully chosen</u> items (chocolate, sweets, magazines, vouchers) are put on display in the hope that you'll <u>eventually</u> be tempted while you're queuing.

## *Celebrity or Brand Endorsement Can Increase Sales*

1) Some companies use <u>endorsement</u> by <u>celebrity chefs</u> to <u>boost sales</u> — the chef's name is used to convince you that it's a quality product.

2) Food companies may partner up with big <u>film or TV brands</u> like 'Space Wars' — using 'Space Wars' on their products or adverts helps target certain <u>age groups</u>.

3) Food companies may <u>sponsor</u> sports and sportspersons, e.g. an energy drink company might sponsor a televised car rally. They'll <u>pay money</u> to put their name on advertising banners, cars, helmets, ... and benefit from it being seen by a <u>wide audience</u>.

## *Companies May Use Health Claims...*

1) Food manufacturers may <u>promote</u> their food as having certain <u>health benefits</u> (e.g. high in vitamin C, 2 of your 5 a day). Claims that make a product appear <u>healthy</u> can <u>greatly increase sales</u>.

2) Manufacturers may also market a <u>low sugar</u> or <u>low fat</u> version of an <u>existing</u> product (e.g. diet cola), or one that only uses <u>natural</u> ingredients in order to attract buyers who are <u>health conscious</u>.

3) Special products such as <u>gluten-free</u> breads target customers who have specific dietary requirements.

## *...or Promote Their Ethical Values*

1) Food companies may join ethical schemes like <u>Fairtrade</u> — it may cost them more to produce the food, but they can charge a <u>higher price</u> and the product will appeal to a <u>wider market</u>.

2) <u>Organic</u> food ranges may be produced to target certain groups — again, it'll cost more to produce, but the customers they're aiming at will probably be willing to pay a <u>higher price</u> for it.

3) Companies may advertise that they use <u>biodegradable</u> or <u>recycled materials</u> in their packaging, to attract customers concerned about the environment.

4) Product labels may use words like '<u>natural</u>' and '<u>fresh</u>' and use images of nature to make the product appear more natural (sometimes hiding the fact that they're actually full of artificial <u>chemicals</u>...).

---

### *You can go large for just 50p...* and have enough popcorn to feed a small country...

Learn all of the sneaky marketing techniques on this page, then give these questions a try.

Q1  Give two ways an existing product can be tweaked in order to be sold as a healthy alternative. [2 marks]

Q2  Why may manufacturers use film franchises to promote their products? [2 marks]

---

# Sensory Testing

What would you rather eat — a cupcake that smells like old cheese or a packet of crunchy roast-dinner flavoured mealworms? We use a combination of senses to try and figure out what we should eat.

## Humans Taste by Using Their Tongue and Nose

1) Human tongues are covered in thousands of taste buds, which detect five different things — salt, sweet, sour, bitter and umami (savoury).

2) We use taste buds in conjunction with olfactory receptors in the nose (which detect smells) to identify the flavour of foods.

*This is why you can't taste food properly when your nose is blocked.*

## Our Senses Influence Our Choice of Food

1) People use a combination of senses to decide whether a food is appetising.

2) Good food should appeal to the senses: sight, smell, taste and touch.

3) Each sense influences food choice in a different way:

**Sight**
We want food that looks appealing, e.g. that's colourful, looks fresh, is attractively presented... not a brown splodge on a plate.

**Taste**
Foods must have an enjoyable taste. The method of cooking, freshness of ingredients, choice of herbs, seasoning and flavour combinations all affect the overall taste.

**Touch**
Texture can make a surprising difference. We like our veg to be crunchy (not chewy and bendy), rice and pasta firm (not soggy), and 'wheat-biscuit' cereals with a little crunch (unless you're one of those strange people who leaves it to go soggy).

**Smell**
Smell helps us to taste food, and can also make us want to eat it (think of the smell of bread baking in the oven... or of chips... mmm). As above, how it's cooked and flavoured will affect the aromas that are given off.

4) For top marks, you'll need to use sensory descriptors to correctly describe the sensory qualities (how a food looks, tastes, feels and smells) for a range of foods and combinations.

Colourful   Crispy   Sour
Sweet   Tender   Crumbly
Firm   Smooth   Chewy

## Make Your Sensory Test Fair and Unbiased

Behind many a great food product is a great sensory test. Sensory testing helps you understand how other people feel about the sensory qualities of your product, so you can go away and improve it.

Here is how a fair and unbiased sensory test should be set up:

1) Choose enough tasters for your tasting panel (e.g. 10).

2) Tasters should not be told what each sample is — this is known as a 'blind test'.

3) Tasters should work on their own, so they cannot be influenced by others.

4) Tasters should be given clear instructions on what they need to do.

5) Only small samples should be given to the tasters, to stop them filling up before the final samples.

6) Tasters should be allowed to drink water between samples to wash the taste away.

7) The tests should be carried out in:
   - Clean, hygienic conditions.
   - A quiet area.
   - Similar testing areas with the same lighting, so that the food looks the same for each tester.

8) When testing is finished, the results can be analysed to see which sensory qualities of the product need improving.

# Sensory Testing

This page covers some of the many different <u>sensory tests</u> that can be used — make sure you can use them correctly and choose the one that is most <u>appropriate</u> for your product.

## *Sensory Tests* **Compare** *Sensory Qualities* **of** *Food*

### Ranking Test

Foods are tasted, and the tasters put the foods in <u>order</u> from <u>lowest</u> to <u>highest</u> (e.g. 1-4) for a certain <u>characteristic</u>, e.g. spiciness, sweetness. The ranks for each food are <u>totalled</u> at the end.

| Taster | Sample — Texture | | | |
|---|---|---|---|---|
| | S1 | S2 | S3 | S4 |
| A | 1 | 4 | 3 | 2 |
| B | 2 | 4 | 3 | 1 |
| C | 1 | 3 | 4 | 2 |
| D | 1 | 4 | 2 | 3 |
| Rank total | 5 | 15 | 12 | 8 |
| Rank place | 4th | 1st | 2nd | 3rd |

### Triangle Test

A <u>triangle test</u> is a type of '<u>discrimination</u>' test. <u>Three</u> food products are tasted, where <u>two</u> are the <u>same</u> and one has a <u>tweaked recipe</u>. The taster has to <u>identify</u> which product <u>differs</u> from the others.

Yup, I think cake B is the odd one out.

### Paired Preference Test

In a <u>paired</u> preference test, <u>two slightly different</u> foods, e.g. two cookies (one made with <u>butter</u> and one made with <u>margarine</u>), are tasted and the taster chooses their <u>favourite</u>.

### (Hedonic) Rating Test

In a hedonic <u>rating test</u>, people rate a <u>variety</u> of foods using a <u>scale</u>, e.g. 1-5, Hate-Love, or smiley face to sad face.

### Profiling Test

Tasters rate certain <u>characteristics</u> of a food and the <u>average</u> rating for each characteristic is worked out to create a <u>profile</u> of the food. This can be displayed visually, e.g. on a star diagram.

| Characteristic | Taster Ratings | | | | Average |
|---|---|---|---|---|---|
| | A | B | C | D | |
| Sourness | 5 | 3 | 2 | 4 | 3.5 |
| Sweetness | 2 | 3 | 2 | 1 | 2 |
| Saltiness | 0 | 1 | 1 | 2 | 1 |
| Spiciness | 5 | 3 | 2 | 3 | 3.25 |

Overlapping two star diagrams lets you easily compare two different foods at a glance, e.g. here, food A is rated more sour, but less sweet and salty than food B.

Key:
Food A
Food B

(star diagram with axes: Sourness, Sweetness, Spiciness, Saltiness)

## *And in first place... the runner beans...*

If you're doing a sensory test, you need to make sure that you're not influencing the tasters' decisions. Go through everything on these pages, then cover them up and write down as much as you can.

Q1    Write down three rules that must be followed in a fair sensory test.    [3 marks]

Q2    Create a table for a profiling test where four people test characteristics of a new scone recipe.    [3 marks]

# Revision Questions for Section Five

Another day, another section.  By now you should be a pro when it comes to understanding food choices, so:

- Try these questions and <u>tick off each one</u> when you <u>get it right</u>.
- When you've done <u>all the questions</u> for a topic and are <u>completely happy</u> with it, tick off the topic.

## Influences on Food Choice (p.60-63) ☐

1) Describe how the following factors influence people's food choices:
   a) cost of food       b) seasonality       c) availability       d) special occasions       e) enjoyment  ☑

2) Outline the dietary laws of:
   a) Hinduism          b) Islam          c) Judaism  ☑

3) Describe how the following factors influence people's food choices:
   a) animal welfare       b) environmental impact  ☑

4) Write down three symptoms of a food intolerance.  ☑

5) Write down four common allergens.  ☑

## Food Labelling and Nutritional Information (p.64-65) ☑

6) Identify one piece of information below that is not compulsory on food labels.
   - How to store the product
   - A 'use by' or 'best before' date
   - The product name
   - Cooking instructions
   - The name and address of the manufacturer
   - A warning if any ingredients are unsuitable for vegetarians
   - A warning if any GM ingredients have been used
   - A list of ingredients (including additives and allergens)  ☑

7) As of December 2016, what compulsory information must be shown in a table on food labels?  ☑

8) What does each colour represent in traffic-light labelling?  ☑

## Influences of Marketing (p.66) ☑

9) Give two examples of special offers that may be used to increase food sales.  ☑

10) Explain how data collected from loyalty card schemes can be used by supermarkets.  ☑

11) Explain how celebrities and film / TV brands can be used to boost sales of food products.  ☑

12) Why might a food company choose to sponsor a sporting event?  ☑

13) How could a manufacturer modify an existing product to attract:
    a) health conscious customers
    b) customers worried about the environment?  ☐

## Sensory Testing (p.67-68) ☐

14) What are the five basic tastes?  ☑

15) Describe how we identify flavours in food.  ☑

16) What is meant by a 'sensory quality' of a food?  ☑

17) Describe how you would make a sensory test fair and unbiased.  ☑

18) Describe how to carry out the following sensory tests:
    a) ranking test     b) triangle test     c) paired preference test  ☑

19) Draw a star diagram to visually represent the
    food profile shown in the table on the right.  ☑

| Characteristic | Taster Ratings | | | | Average |
|---|---|---|---|---|---|
| | A | B | C | D | |
| Crunchiness | 3 | 5 | 4 | 4 | 4 |
| Bitterness | 3 | 2 | 2 | 1 | 2 |
| Dryness | 5 | 4 | 4 | 5 | 4.5 |

# Practical Skills

**A note about this section**

On these pages we'll cover all the <u>practical skills</u> you need to learn for Eduqas.
You should have practised all these skills during your course — this is just a <u>brief reminder</u>.
If there are any that you're <u>rusty</u> on, it's time to do some <u>brushing up</u>.

- Make sure you have a <u>detailed knowledge</u> and <u>understanding</u> of all of these skills for your <u>exam</u>.
- You'll also need to <u>demonstrate a good range</u> of these skills in your <u>non-exam assessment</u>.

## Skill 1: Knife Skills

### Different Knives are Used for Different Jobs

You need a variety of <u>knives</u> for all the <u>different skills</u> you use when preparing food:

A <u>cook's knife</u> is useful for <u>chopping</u>.

A <u>vegetable knife</u> is suitable for <u>cutting small pieces of food</u>.

A <u>filleting knife</u> is used for removing fillets of meat and fish.

A <u>boning knife</u> is handy for <u>removing bones</u> from large joints of meat.

It's <u>REALLY IMPORTANT</u> to take care when using these knives as they can cause serious harm.

### There are Different Ways to Cut Fruit and Vegetables

1) When cutting <u>smaller fruits and vegetables</u> (e.g. apples or potatoes) use a <u>bridge hold</u>.

2) When cutting <u>longer fruits and vegetables</u> (e.g. carrots or cucumbers) use a <u>claw grip</u>. It's really important that your <u>fingers</u> are <u>tucked under</u> here so they don't get sliced off.

3) You can use a knife to <u>peel</u>, <u>slice</u> and <u>dice</u> (chop into small cubes) your fruit and veg. Or cut them into <u>batons</u> (thick sticks) or, to be fancier, <u>julienne</u> strips (thin sticks).

### Cutting Meat and Fish is More Complicated

1) Cutting meat and fish is more complicated and requires a different approach to cutting fruit and veg. It also requires a different type of knife, e.g. a <u>boning</u> or <u>filleting knife</u> (see above).

2) You can <u>divide</u> a <u>whole chicken</u> into eight portions (two of each of the following: drumsticks, thighs, breasts and wings). The chicken breasts are then often <u>filleted</u> (this removes the skin and tenderloin).

3) Different methods of filleting are needed for <u>round</u> fish (e.g. mackerel) and <u>flatfish</u> (e.g. plaice) due to the position of the backbone. You'll typically get 2 fillets (pieces) from round fish, and 4 from flatfish.

4) Knives can be used to remove <u>fat</u> and <u>rind</u> (the thick skin of foods such as pork).

> There are loads of video tutorials online that show you how to portion and fillet various foods with step-by-step instructions.

# Practical Skills

## Skill 2: Prepare Fruit and Vegetables

1) You probably already know (and use) lots of the different ways you can prepare fruit and veg.

2) Some of the most common include: mashing, crushing, shredding, grating, peeling, de-seeding and blending.

3) Other methods include:

Blanching, scooping, de-skinning — sounds like something from a horror movie to me...

- Segmenting — e.g. dividing an orange into segments.
- Piping — e.g. piping mash to create decorative patterns.
- Blanching — placing the fruit or veg into boiling then cold water (see p.25).
- De-skinning — this can be done by blanching tomatoes (after blanching, the skins can be peeled off easily just using your fingertips).
- Scooping — this is used when balling melons or making equal portions of mash.
- Juicing — e.g. using a lemon squeezer.
- Preparing garnishes — e.g. tomato roses that go alongside a main dish.
- Scissor snipping — e.g. when snipping herbs. You can use special herb scissors that have multiple blades to make snipping even quicker.

4) You can also prevent enzymic browning while preparing fruit and veg, e.g. by blanching them or adding an acid like lemon juice (see p.37).

## Skill 3: Prepare, Combine and Shape

1) You can shape and bind wet mixtures by hand, e.g. shaping burgers, fish cakes, meatballs, or doughs for biscuits or bread buns — it's quick, but your results might not be very consistent.

2) You can also combine different foods in a variety of ways to make your dishes more interesting:

Chickens in blankets anyone?

- You can wrap foods around each other — e.g. wrapping bacon around chicken or sausages.
- Foods including meat, vegetables and fruit can be skewered together to make kebabs.
- Different types of rolls can be made — e.g. sushi, sausage rolls and spring rolls.
- You can coat foods with different ingredients — e.g. coating chicken pieces, fish or cheese by covering them in flour, then egg, then breadcrumbs.
- Foods can also be combined by layering them. A popular example is lasagne, although layering can also be achieved more simply — e.g. the mashed potato on the top of a shepherd's pie.

Vegetable kebab

Maki roll

Chicken in breadcrumbs

Lasagne

## Shape it! Mix it! Roll it! Bind it!

Experimenting with how you can shape, combine and cook food is a heck of a lot of fun. Without the invention of unusual ideas, we wouldn't have the delicious combinations we have today — chocolate on pizza, for example.

# Practical Skills

Now if this stuff doesn't get you excited, I don't know what will. Seriously though, this stuff is dead useful.

## Skill 4: Tenderise and Marinate

1) Marination involves soaking vegetables, meat, fish or alternatives such as tofu in a liquid before they're cooked. This liquid often contains herbs, spices and acid (e.g. lemon juice).

2) The acid in marinades makes meat more tender by denaturing protein (see p.29).

3) Marinades also add flavour and moisture to food. It's common for foods such as chicken to be paired with barbecue, sweet chilli or tandoori marinades.

Marinated tofu changes colour as it absorbs the marinade.

## Skill 5: Select and Adjust a Cooking Process

1) Cooking time is affected by different factors, including the type of food (e.g. fish cooks a lot faster than red meat) and portion size (e.g. a thick piece of steak needs cooking for longer than a thin one).

2) Select an appropriate cooking time, but be prepared to adapt it — e.g. if your food is cooking quicker than expected, reduce the cooking time (but make sure that you cook it thoroughly all the way through to the middle).

Cakes can sink if you remove them from the oven before they're cooked, if you open the oven during cooking (letting cold air in) or if you put too much sugar in the mixture. These can be prevented by making sure the oven is up to temperature before baking and that each ingredient is measured precisely.

## Skill 6: Weigh and Measure

1) Dry ingredients (e.g. flour) and solid ingredients (e.g. butter) are usually measured with electronic or balance weighing scales.

2) Liquids are measured in measuring jugs or cups (some dry ingredients are measured in cups too), and you can use measuring spoons (e.g. a teaspoon) for small amounts.

## Skill 7: Preparation of Ingredients & Equipment

1) It's a good idea to organise all your ingredients and equipment before you start cooking (e.g. weighing and measuring out your ingredients).

2) You can also grease, oil, line or flour equipment like tins — this not only makes removing the food easier, but it also helps with cleaning up after.

## Skill 8: Use of Equipment

1) Blenders are used to blend (chop and mix) different ingredients together. This makes them good for soups and smoothies. They come in many different forms: some are a jug with a rotating blade, while with others you lower the blade into the food by hand.

2) Food processors are similar to blenders but they can be used for mixing, slicing, chopping, grinding and dicing food. Using the same settings will give you the same results each time. They're good for making burgers, meatballs, quickly chopping onions or (with an attachment) grating carrots.

3) Food mixers (unsurprisingly) mix food. They're often used for making cake mixtures and batters. Like blenders, they can be hand-held or come as a worktop appliance with a mixing bowl attached.

4) Pasta machines have rollers that turn your pasta dough into flat sheets of pasta. They can usually be adjusted to change the thickness of the pasta and create different types of pasta.

5) Microwave ovens use radiation (see p.24) to quickly cook foods such as baked potato and to heat up foods such as baked beans. They're also good for quickly melting foods like chocolate and cheese.

Not to be used as a laundry mangle...

Section Six — Preparation and Cooking Techniques

# Practical Skills

## Skills 9 to 12: Use of the Cooker and Cooking Methods

The technical side of the <u>cooking methods</u> below have been covered in <u>Section 2</u>, but here's a quick recap on how you can use your cooker's <u>grill</u>, <u>oven</u> and <u>hob</u>:

Well hello me!

**Grill**
- The cooker can grill food such as <u>meat</u>, <u>fish</u>, <u>veg</u> and <u>firm cheese</u> like <u>halloumi</u> (see p.27).
- You can also use the grill to <u>char</u> (blacken the outside) and <u>toast</u> foods, e.g. seeds and nuts.

**Oven**
- The <u>oven</u> can be used for <u>baking</u> (p.27), <u>roasting</u> (p.28) and <u>braising</u> (p.26).
- You can also use it to cook <u>casseroles</u> and <u>tagines</u>. Both are <u>slow-cooked</u> to <u>tenderise</u> the meat inside. Like braising, they cook food in a mix of liquid, vegetables and herbs. A <u>tagine</u> is a <u>slow-cooked North African dish</u> that's cooked in a covered pot which (confusingly) is also called a tagine. Both casseroles and tagines are <u>covered</u> during cooking to trap moisture.

A tagine... in... a tagine

**Hob**
- <u>Water-based</u> hob methods include <u>steaming</u>, <u>boiling</u>, <u>simmering</u>, <u>blanching</u> and <u>poaching</u> (p.25).
- <u>Fat-based</u> hob methods include <u>stir-frying</u> and <u>shallow frying</u> (p.26).
- The hob is also used for <u>dry frying</u>, sometimes called <u>dry roasting</u> (p.28).

## Skill 13: Make Sauces

### Sauces can be Made in Lots of Different Ways

Sauces are used in both savoury and sweet dishes — as an <u>accompaniment</u> (e.g. custard, ketchup) or as <u>part</u> of the dish (e.g. in lasagne). You can put pretty much anything you like in a sauce, but they usually contain at least one of these: <u>flour</u>, <u>butter</u>, <u>eggs</u>, <u>cornflour</u>, <u>stock</u>, <u>milk</u>, <u>cream</u>, <u>sugar</u>. Here are three ways you can make a sauce:

> When making a sauce, heat is transferred by <u>conduction</u> (from the pan to the sauce) and <u>convection</u> (through the sauce) — see p.24.

### Gelatinisation Thickens Starch-Based Sauces

Starch-based sauces thicken by <u>gelatinisation</u> (see p.30). They can be made in different ways:

You can make a <u>roux</u> as a base for your sauce by mixing equal weights of <u>melted butter</u> and <u>plain flour</u> in a pan — stir until the flour is <u>cooked</u> (to add colour and get rid of the raw flour taste). Gradually add <u>liquid</u> (e.g. milk) to make a sauce, stirring to avoid lumps the whole time. <u>Simmer</u>, then add the rest of your ingredients. The roux will help to give your sauce a good <u>consistency</u> (thickness) and <u>flavour</u>.

To make a <u>blended sauce</u>, you mix <u>cornflour</u> with a small amount of <u>water/milk</u> to form a paste (a blend of starch and liquid). You then heat up additional liquid and add it to the paste to make a sauce. <u>Heat</u> the sauce until it <u>thickens</u>.

Or you can just make an <u>all-in-one</u> sauce by putting all your ingredients into a saucepan. <u>Stir</u> over a medium heat, until your sauce starts to bubble and thicken.

You can <u>infuse</u> a plain roux sauce with other ingredients to make a <u>velouté</u> sauce or a <u>béchamel</u> sauce:

- A <u>velouté sauce</u> is made by adding <u>white stock</u> (e.g. chicken or fish stock) to the roux <u>instead of milk</u>.
- For a <u>béchamel sauce</u>, you simmer the milk with foods such as <u>peppercorns</u>, <u>onions</u>, <u>cloves</u> and <u>bay leaves</u>.

The <u>thickness</u> of your sauce depends on the <u>ratio of starch to liquid</u> in it, e.g. the more milk you add to your roux, the thinner your sauce will become. This has many different uses, such as using a <u>thick</u> roux sauce to <u>bind ingredients</u> together in a fish cake, or making a <u>thin pouring sauce</u>, e.g. a cheese sauce.

Starch-based sauces can often become lumpy, e.g. if the liquid is added too quickly or the mixture isn't stirred (agitated) enough, so it's important to add the liquid gradually and stir thoroughly. You can sometimes save a lumpy sauce by using a sieve to get rid of any larger lumps.

# Practical Skills

## Reduction Sauces *Thicken by Evaporation*

You can include liquids like cooking juices, stock and wine in reduction sauces.

1) Reduction is a process that <u>thickens liquids</u> such as <u>sauces</u> and soups by <u>simmering</u> them and causing water to <u>evaporate</u> — this also <u>concentrates</u> the <u>flavour</u> of the sauce, making it more <u>intense</u>.

2) Common reduction sauces include <u>tomato pasta sauce</u>, <u>curry sauce</u> and <u>gravy</u>, although they can also be sweet-tasting — such as apple or raspberry <u>coulis</u>.

## Emulsion Sauces *Contain Oil and Water*

There's loads of stuff about <u>emulsion sauces</u> (e.g. hollandaise) on p.32.

## Skill 14: *Set a Mixture — Removal of Heat (Gelation)*

1) Foods such as custard or ice cream set when they are <u>chilled</u> or <u>frozen</u>.

2) This process is called <u>gelation</u> — this also happens with unbaked cheesecakes, as they need to be <u>left in the fridge</u> overnight to set.

3) It's easy to get confused between gelation and gelatinisation (p.30) — remember, <u>gelation</u> involves <u>chilling</u>, while <u>gelatinisation</u> involves <u>heating</u>.

## Skill 15: *Set a Mixture — Heating (Coagulation)*

1) Mixtures that contain <u>egg</u> (e.g. quiches or egg custards) can be set by <u>heating</u>.

2) This is because when they're cooked, heat causes the <u>proteins</u> in the eggs to <u>denature</u> and <u>coagulate</u> (see p.29).

3) It's this <u>coagulation</u> of proteins in the mixture that causes it to set — it also traps the other ingredients in the mixture, e.g. bacon in quiche.

## Skill 16: *Use of Raising Agents*

Raising agents (see p.33) come in many <u>different forms</u>:

- <u>Chemical</u> (bicarbonate of soda, baking powder and self-raising flour), <u>biological</u> (yeast), <u>mechanical</u> (folding, beating, whisking, sieving, creaming and rubbing in) and <u>steam</u>.

- <u>Eggs</u> can be used as a raising agent as their proteins stretch and trap air when they are whisked — this creates a gas-in-liquid <u>foam</u> that solidifies when the food is cooked (p.29).

Remember, using too little (or too much) of a raising agent can cause a cake to sink.

## Skill 17: *Make a Dough*

1) You need to make doughs whenever you make foods like <u>bread</u>, <u>pastry</u> and <u>pasta</u>.

2) Most doughs are made by combining <u>flour</u>, <u>water</u> and a bit of <u>salt</u>.

3) If you're making <u>pasta dough</u>, you can <u>change the water for eggs</u>.

4) <u>Bread doughs</u> also include <u>yeast</u> to give the final product a nice <u>rise</u> (p.33).

5) <u>Fat</u> or <u>oil</u> is added to change the <u>texture</u> of the dough — loads of it is used in pastry, and just a little in bread or pasta.

6) Making doughs can show you've learned lots of <u>technical skills</u>, including:

- <u>Shortening</u> (see p.31), e.g. if you were making shortcrust pastry.
- <u>Forming gluten</u> (see p.29), e.g. if you were kneading bread dough.
- <u>Proving</u> (see p.33), e.g. if you were making risen bread.

# Practical Skills

## Different Types of Pastry Have Different Properties

When making <u>pastry dough</u>, you need to choose which one gives you the right <u>taste</u> and <u>texture</u>:

| Type of pastry | Properties of finished pastry | Used for... |
|---|---|---|
| Shortcrust | A 'short' texture (see p.31) | pies, quiches, tarts and pasties |
| Sweet | Sweeter than other pastries | sweet pies and tarts |
| Puff | Has flaky, puffed up layers | sausage rolls, pies, fruit turnovers |
| Choux | Light texture and hollow centre | profiteroles and eclairs |
| Filo | Light, crisp and fragile | strudels and pastry parcels |

Choux!

Each dough is different, and you need to think about different things for each one. E.g. when making <u>choux pastry</u> (for which the dough is more like a paste than other doughs), you need to <u>cool</u> the hot flour/butter mixture <u>before</u> adding your <u>eggs</u> (to avoid protein coagulation), and make sure you use enough water and a hot oven so that steam can be created and make the dough rise.

## Skill 18: Shaping and Finishing a Dough

When it comes to adding <u>shape</u> and <u>finishing touches</u> to your dough, there are a lot of options. Here's a big list of ways you could shape and finish your dough. You should know what each one is and be ready to <u>demonstrate some</u> in your <u>non-exam assessment task</u>.

- You can <u>roll out</u> doughs to get the right <u>shape</u> and <u>thickness</u>. Use a <u>rolling pin</u> to get an even thickness, and <u>flour</u> to stop the mixture sticking to surfaces.
- <u>Folding</u> a dough creates layers. This helps to trap air (p.33) and is used to make foods like puff pastries and palmiers.
- You can <u>line cases</u> with pastry dough (press the dough into the shape of the case — the dough then bakes into this shape, giving your pie a solid <u>pastry case</u>. You can prick the pastry with a fork to release any air and keep a flat base.

Palmiers

Lining a pastry tin

- <u>Bread rolls</u> can be shaped in a <u>huge variety</u> of ways, including: baguettes, bloomers, rings, bagels, cobs, braids, breadsticks, rolls etc...
- You can make different types of <u>flatbread</u> — lots of them don't use yeast (e.g. <u>tortillas</u>), although it's sometimes added to give them a relatively small rise (e.g. <u>naan bread</u>).

- <u>Choux pastry</u> is used to make foods like <u>profiteroles</u> and <u>chocolate eclairs</u> — you can <u>pipe</u> it in different ways and shapes to create different products.
- <u>Pasta dough</u> can be shaped in lots of different ways to give us pasta like: ravioli, lasagne, cannelloni, tagliatelle, tortellini etc...
- Dough can be made into <u>pinwheels</u> by rolling it (not with a rolling pin, but in the same way you'd roll up a carpet). Cinnamon buns and cheesy pinwheels are made this way — you can even make coloured swirls by adding fillings.
- The most common shape for a pizza base is circular with thicker crusts around the outside. You can also make a <u>calzone</u> by <u>folding</u> the pizza over, completely covering the filling with dough.

- The shape of doughs change during <u>proving</u> as they <u>rise</u> and increase in size.
- Brushing your doughs with <u>egg wash</u> (egg mixed with water, milk or cream) creates a nice <u>glaze</u> that turns the food <u>golden brown</u> during baking.
- You can also finish the tops of pies and tarts using <u>decorative patterns</u> (p.76).

# Practical Skills

## Skill 19: Test for Readiness

You need to be able to tell if food is <u>cooked through</u> properly. Luckily, there are ways to check this:

- <u>Temperature probes</u> are placed into the middle of food to check if it's <u>hot enough</u> (see p.40).
- You can pop <u>knives</u> or <u>skewers</u> into food such as cake mixtures — if they come out <u>clean</u> then the mixture is cooked.
- You can also cut into <u>meats</u> and apply a little pressure — if the <u>juices</u> come out <u>clear</u> (without blood) the food is cooked.
- You can <u>gently press</u> cakes — they <u>spring back</u> if they're cooked.
- When cooking foods like pasta, you can <u>bite</u> into a small piece to see if it's cooked to your liking. But be warned — too much use of the bite test can quickly result in small meals.
- If you've ever baked biscuits until they were '<u>golden brown</u>', you've successfully completed a <u>visual colour check</u>.
- You can also perform a <u>sound check</u> by knocking on the bottom of baked bread — if it's baked correctly you should hear a hollow sound.

Testing Testing, 1, 2, 3

## Skill 20: Judge and Manipulate Sensory Properties

### Change How Food Affects the Senses

1) You can change the flavour of foods with <u>salt</u>, <u>pepper</u>, <u>sugar</u>, <u>herbs</u> and <u>spices</u>, but also by using:

- <u>Pastes</u> (e.g. garlic paste)
- <u>Reductions</u> (see p.74)
- <u>Jus</u> (a thin sauce made from the juices of cooked meat)
- <u>Infused oils</u> (oils that have absorbed the flavour of herbs)

When cooking, try a small amount of your food to see how it tastes. You can then adjust it until the flavour is right.

2) The <u>texture</u> of food can be changed by adding <u>crust</u>, <u>crispiness</u> and <u>crumbs</u>, e.g. coating chicken in breadcrumbs, adding seeds to bread dough or breadcrumbs on top of a dish, e.g. macaroni cheese.

3) <u>Browning</u> changes the <u>flavour</u> and <u>appearance</u> of food:

- Both <u>dextrinisation</u> and <u>caramelisation</u> brown food (see p.30).
- You can even use a cook's <u>blowtorch</u> to brown the tops of foods, e.g. a crème brûlée.
- You can <u>glaze</u> foods (e.g. pies) by <u>brushing egg</u> over the food. When it cooks, the pie will have a nice golden brown colour.

Jeff always wanted to be a painter...

### Add Garnishes and Decorate Your Dishes

1) <u>Garnishes</u> are small <u>additions</u> to your dish and can <u>add extra colour</u> and/or <u>flavour</u>. These can be as <u>simple or complicated</u> as you want, from a slice of lemon or a piece of lettuce to a piped balsamic sauce or a flower made out of a radish.

2) Other <u>decorative techniques</u> can be used, such as <u>piping</u> icing onto a cake, or creating a decorative <u>pattern</u> on top of a pie.

3) Styling your food using these techniques can make your dish look <u>more appealing</u>.

---

## I heard this joke about margherita pizza — it was so cheesy...

All these skills might seem a little overwhelming at first, but if you go through them one at a time it will get easier.

# Skills Checklist

So long <u>section 6</u> — there are a lot of practical skills on these pages, but it's important you can use them.
- Go through this list of practical skills and <u>tick off each one</u> when you <u>can do it</u>.
- When you can do <u>all the parts</u> of a skill section and are <u>completely happy</u> with it, tick it off.

### Skill 1: Knife Skills (p.70) ☑

1) I can safely use different knives for different uses. ☑
2) I can cut fruit and vegetables in different ways. ☑
3) I know how chicken and fish can be portioned. ☑

### Skills 2-3: Preparing, Combining and Shaping (p.71) ☑

4) I can prepare fruit and vegetables in many different ways. ☑
5) I can prepare, shape and combine foods in a variety of ways. ☑

### Skill 4: Tenderise and Marinate (p.72) ☑

6) I can make marinades to tenderise and flavour food. ☑

### Skills 5-7 : General Practical Skills (p.72) ☑

7) I can select and adapt cooking times. ☑
8) I can weigh and measure ingredients accurately. ☑
9) I can organise all my ingredients before cooking. ☑

### Skill 8: Use of Equipment (p.72) ☑

10) I can use different equipment to speed up food preparation processes and save time. ☑

### Skills 9-12: Use of the Cooker and Cooking Methods (p.73) ☑

11) I can use the oven, grill and hob on the cooker for a range of cooking methods. ☑

### Skill 13: Sauce Making (p.73-74) ☑

12) I can make a roux, blended and all-in-one sauce. ☑
13) I can adapt a roux sauce to make a velouté and béchamel sauce. ☑
14) I can make both sweet and savoury reduction sauces. ☑
15) I can make a stable emulsion sauce. ☑

### Skills 14-15: Setting Mixtures (p.74) ☑

16) I can set mixtures using gelation. ☑
17) I can set mixtures using eggs. ☑

### Skill 16: Raising Agents (p.74) ☑

18) I can use different raising agents to make my food rise. ☑

### Skills 17-18: Making, Shaping and Finishing Dough (p.74-75) ☑

19) I can make a variety of different doughs using shortening, gluten formation and fermentation. ☑
20) I can select the right type of pastry dough for my dish. ☑
21) I can shape and finish my dough in lots of different ways. ☑

### Skills 19-20: Testing for Readiness and Changing Sensory Properties (p.76) ☑

22) I can test food in a variety of ways to see if it's cooked. ☑
23) I can change how food affects the different senses. ☑
24) I can add garnishes and decoration to my food. ☑

# Non-Exam Assessment Advice

In Food Preparation & Nutrition you'll have to do some cooking... and it'll be worth a good portion of the marks.

## The Non-Exam Tasks are Worth 50% of the Total Marks

1) During the final year of your GCSE, you'll have to do some non-exam tasks.
They allow you to show off your culinary knowledge and cooking skills.

2) The non-exam work is split into two parts — a Food Investigation task worth 30 marks (15% of the course), and a Food Preparation task worth 70 marks (35% of the course).

## The Food Investigation Task Involves Some Experimenting

1) In the Food Investigation task, you'll have to investigate and write a report about how and why ingredients work in a chosen task, e.g. "Investigate the ingredients used in sweet scone baking."

2) You'll be marked on three main things — research, investigation and analysis.

### A — Research

1) Read your task thoroughly, then make a plan of action (e.g. a mind map of things you want to research) — particularly how ingredients work, and why.

2) Use a range of sources to research your ideas, including textbooks, the Internet and your own knowledge.

3) Use this research to make a prediction you can investigate — e.g. "Self-raising flour will be the best raising agent to use for making sweet scones."

### B — Investigation

1) To test your prediction you'll need to plan some practical investigations. You need to carry out several experiments (e.g. making scones with different flours, mechanically aerating scones in different ways).

2) It's important that these experiments have clear methods and are fair.

3) Prepare any tables or graphs to record your results in beforehand — this will make it clear what you need to write down during the experiments.

4) You should also take photos throughout your experiments to prove what you did.

- E.g. Cook all at the same temperature, for the same length of time.
- Make sure all ingredients are weighed accurately.
- Make all scones the same size by using a cutter or weighing scale.

### C — Analysis/Evaluation

1) You'll then need to analyse and evaluate your findings (interpret what you've discovered).

2) You can do this by linking your findings to the research you did at the start of the task (explaining how and why your ingredients worked the way they did), discussing your results, and deciding whether your findings support your prediction (is what happened what you expected?).

3) You need to show that you've done all this by producing a written report. This will include:

- A summary of your research (including how it helped you understand the task).
- Your prediction (including how your research led you to this decision).
- The aims of your different experiments (what you hoped to achieve).
- The ingredients you used in your experiments.
- The methods you used in your experiments and how you made each one a fair test.
- The results of your experiments (include any tables/graphs/charts here).
- Any photos you took during the task.
- An analysis of your results (this should fully explain what you have learned from them).
- A conclusion — this should sum up what you've learned, looking at your original predictions, results, how you'd apply what you've learned to future cooking projects, and any further research you'd do if you had the chance.

You really want to show off your knowledge here, so remember to use correct technical terms.

# Non-Exam Assessment Advice

## The Food Preparation Task Involves Lots of Cooking

1) In the Food Preparation task you'll have to cook a range of dishes to fit a chosen task, as well as producing a portfolio to show the following things:

- Your research (finding out more about your chosen task).
- Your use of planning and practical skills (e.g. different technical skills/cooking techniques).
- Your ability to prepare, cook and present three dishes within a period of 3 hours.
- An analysis and evaluation of your chosen dishes.

2) During the practical tasks you should take photographs of each stage in the preparation and cooking. You will use these photographs in your portfolio.

## Part 1 — Doing the Research

1) First, make sure you've read both tasks properly, then choose the one you find most appealing. Each task on the brief has a certain research focus, such as 'dietary requirements', 'lifestyle choices' or 'specific contexts'. E.g. "A local school is planning a week where only vegan meals are served in the canteen. Research, prepare and cook three dishes the canteen could serve that week."

2) Decide what you need to research. This could be stuff like:

- Advantages and disadvantages of a vegan diet.
- Meat and dairy-free alternatives to everyday food products, and their nutritional values, e.g. soya milk, sunflower spread.
- Surveying vegans to ask about their personal food choices and / or the availability of vegan products.
- Nutritional guidelines for vegans.

Not that kind of survey Neville. Always make sure your research is relevant to the brief.

3) Carry out your research, then summarise what you've found on a page of your portfolio. You can then use this research to help you plan your dishes.

## Part 2 — Making Trial Dishes

1) In this part, you'll need to plan and cook a few trial dishes using the information you found in part 1. What you find out during these trial dishes will help you select your final three dishes.

2) It's useful to create a plan of action here, making notes about everything you want to accomplish. One helpful task is making a mind map of dishes that fit your brief. You can narrow down your choices by making a list of important things your dishes should achieve, such as:

- Do my dishes agree with my task and research findings?
- Am I capable of making the dishes to a high standard under timed conditions?
- Do the dishes show off enough technical skills? E.g. making a dough, making a sauce.
- How much will the dishes cost to make, and will I be able to find the ingredients?

3) When you've chosen your trial dishes, write a brief summary of the technical skills required for each.

4) Make sure you take plenty of photographs whilst you're making the dishes (especially when carrying out technical skills) — you'll need to put these in your portfolio to prove what you've done.

5) There are lots of ways you can structure this part of your portfolio, but remember to talk about why you chose each dish, the skills you've used for each dish, and a list of ingredients — don't forget to pop in those photographs you took too.

*You need to work hygienically and safely when cooking these dishes, or you'll lose marks (or a finger).*

80

# Non-Exam Assessment Advice

## Part 3 — Planning and Making the Final Dishes

1) Next, you'll have to plan and justify your choices for the final three dishes.

2) Give a written explanation for each dish you plan to make. Say how they fit the task, any technical skills you'll use, plus any further reasoning (e.g. how your trial dishes influenced your choices or if the results of any sensory tests have led to new ideas).

*You could make three main courses, or you could make a starter, main and dessert.*

3) On the day, you'll have three hours to prepare, cook and present all three dishes, so you'll need a time plan to keep you on track.

4) Make a time plan that's easy to understand, and include timings, what you need to do at each stage, and any food safety notes.

| Time | What I need to do | Notes / Health & Safety |
|---|---|---|
| 9:00 | Weigh out my flour, salt, cheese, spinach (etc.) for my ravioli dish. | Wipe surfaces with antibacterial cleaner beforehand (and after handling any raw ingredients). |
| 9:15 | Start preparing the shortcrust pastry for my apple pie by rubbing the butter and the flour together. | Make sure to wash my hands after weighing out the ravioli ingredients. |

5) You'll need to "dovetail" your three dishes to get them finished in the three hours you have — this means that rather than making each dish in order from start to finish, you'll have to keep working on all three dishes across the three hour period.

6) Be sure to take photos of your dishes, both during the process and as finished dishes.

### You'll be Assessed on...

- Your use of technical skills and equipment.
- Your ability to follow food safety rules.
- Your use and understanding of a wide range of ingredients.
- Your use of cooking times and different cooking methods.
- Your ability to test for readiness.

- Your ability to judge and adjust the sensory properties of your dishes during cooking.
- Your use of a good time plan and dovetailing.
- Your use of good portion control.
- Your presentation and any finishing touches you added to your dishes.
- The complexity of your dishes.

## Part 4 — Analysis and Evaluation of Your Final Dishes

1) This is the last bit — hooray! You'll need to write up a detailed analysis of your final dishes.

2) Your analysis should be tailored to your chosen brief, but don't forget to include stuff like:

- A sensory test of the finished dishes. Make sure you use the correct sensory descriptors here.
- A review of the technical skills used.

- Any modifications you made during the task.
- Any improvements that could be made. Comparing your dishes with other students' can be helpful here.

3) Here's a (very brief) example of how you could structure your analysis. Yours should include much more detail though — the more detail, explanation and description you add the better:

**Analysis:** Vegan ravioli with a spicy tomato sauce
*I presented my handmade ravioli with a spicy tomato sauce, and the dish was finished off with sprigs of parsley... (etc.)*

**Sensory Test:**
*Aroma scored most highly (33/40). This is likely due to the herbs and onions I added to my tomato sauce... (etc.)*

| Characteristic | Taster | | | | |
|---|---|---|---|---|---|
| | A | B | C | D | Total |
| Flavour | 8 | 8 | 7 | 9 | 32 |
| Texture | 6 | 7 | 8 | 8 | 29 |
| Appearance | 5 | 6 | 6 | 6 | 23 |
| Aroma | 9 | 8 | 9 | 7 | 33 |

*However, appearance scored the lowest (23/40), so I should work on making the sauce look more attractive. For example, I could work on making it less lumpy... (etc.)*

**Review of technical skills:**
*I weighed out my ingredients using precise electric scales, and then used an electric food mixer to combine them and make a dough. I kneaded and folded the dough until it was elastic and smooth... (etc.)*

**Presentation:**
*The sauce and parsley garnish (which I finely chopped) adds two different, bold colours to the dish, making it look more appealing... (etc.)*

**Nutritional value:**
*The dish was nutritionally well-balanced. It was low in saturated fats (only 6 g per portion) as it did not contain any butter. It also contained lots of fibre (3.4 g per portion). However, it could be improved by adding more protein... (etc.)*

*You could also include a nutritional info table here (see p.17).*

You can have your own section for modifications and improvements, but you can also incorporate them into your analysis like this.

4) That just leaves the exam to do. Phew...

# Exam Advice

## Here's What to Expect in the Exam

1) At the end of your GCSE Food Preparation and Nutrition course you'll have to sit an exam. It's worth 50% of your total mark.

2) The questions in the exam will test you on all areas of the course — you'll need to know everything in this book for the top marks.

3) The exam is worth 100 marks and is split into two sections:

**Section A**
- In Section A, you'll be given questions related to some 'visual stimuli'.
- The visual stimuli could be a set of images showing a cooking method or the stages of making a dish etc.

**Section B**
- Section B has a variety of questions with different styles and lengths.
- Extended response questions are worth the most marks.

4) The exam is 1 hour and 45 minutes long — you should aim for at least a mark per minute, which will give you some time left over to check your work at the end.

## Remember These Tips

1) **Always** read every question **carefully**.
Don't write an essay about vitamin C if it's asking about vitamin D.

2) **Write your answers clearly**, using good grammar, spelling and punctuation.
If the examiner can't read your answer you won't get any marks, even if it's right.

3) **Underline** any **key words** in the question.
This helps you focus on the important parts that you want to write about.

4) **Use the correct terminology.**
Know your foody terms — GM, CHD, BMR... you can't talk about these if you don't know what they mean.

5) **Don't panic.**
If you really can't do a question, just leave it and move on to the next one. You can come back to it at the end.

## Understand the Command Words

Questions will use command words — they are words that tell you how to answer the question. If you don't know what they mean, you might not answer the question properly.

**State / Identify** You should give a short answer or select an item from a table, a list or similar — you don't need to explain why.

**Define** You should give a clear, precise meaning of the word or phrase.

**Outline** You should give a brief summary of a process.

**Describe** You should give a detailed description of something.

**Explain** You should give reasons to show why.

**Discuss** You should make a balanced argument covering a range of opinions.

**Assess / Evaluate** You should use evidence and your own knowledge to come to a conclusion.

# Exam Advice

## Plan Out Your Answer to Extended Response Questions

Extended response questions are longer questions worth 6 or more marks and with a scary number of dotted lines underneath... They often use command words like discuss, evaluate or assess (see prev pg).

- Your answer must be well-written (good spelling, grammar and punctuation) and well-structured.
- Before you start an extended response question, jot down the points you want to make and plan your answer to help structure it well and avoid repeating things.
- You might have to weigh up the advantages and disadvantages of something, or cover both sides of an argument then form your own opinion.
- Make absolutely sure you're answering the question and not just waffling on.

Here's an example:

7. Evaluate the value of packaging for manufacturers and consumers and discuss ways to limit the impact packaging has on the environment. [8]

> Packaging helps protect and preserve a food product whilst it is being transported and stored, preventing it from being damaged or contaminated, and extending its shelf life. Metal cans, for example, are strong, and are sealed and heated to kill off microorganisms. Correct packaging helps reduce food waste and also helps the manufacturer save money. Packaging is useful for consumers too, as food labels have to include certain information by law (such as allergens and 'use by' dates). This information is particularly valuable for consumers with dietary requirements. For example, coeliacs can check for gluten in the ingredients list and people with religious beliefs can check foods have been prepared in the correct way (e.g. kosher food in Judaism). Manufacturing, transporting and throwing away packaging damages the environment (as this produces greenhouse gases), but there are ways manufacturers and consumers can limit this impact. Manufacturers could limit the use of 'excess' packaging and use recyclable materials, because recycling uses less energy than making new packaging from raw materials. All households in the UK have access to recycling services, so consumers should recycle paper, card, plastics and metal, and should also reuse plastic bags when they go shopping.

*Underline key words in the question — your answer should discuss both of these groups.*

*You'll need a well-structured answer showing detailed knowledge to get all 8 marks.*

*Shows good knowledge of current food labelling practices.*

*The number of lines gives you a good guide to how long your answer should be.*

*This answer has good grammar, spelling and punctuation.*

*Shows good understanding of why this would limit the impact on the environment.*

*This answer has been well planned out.*

Value of packaging
— Manufacturers — Preserves / protects products
— Consumers — food labels — Dietary requirements (medical, beliefs)

Reducing impact
— Manufacturers — Use less ('excess') / Use recyclable materials
— Consumers — Recycle - paper, plastics, metal, card / Reuse plastic bags

# Answers

A note about answers and marks
The answers and mark schemes given here should be used mainly for guidance, as there may be many different correct answers to each question — don't panic if your answers are a bit different.

## Section One — Food, Nutrition and Health

### Pages 1-2 — Proteins
**Q1** Non-essential amino acids can be made by our bodies *[1 mark]*, whereas essential amino acids are the amino acids that our bodies can't make (we have to eat them as part of our diet) *[1 mark]*.

### Pages 3-4 — Fats
**Q1** E.g. bacon *[1 mark]* and butter *[1 mark]*.

**Q2** E.g. Fat-soluble vitamins can't be absorbed by the body, which can lead to a vitamin deficiency *[1 mark]*. It can lead to weight loss (especially if there is also a lack of carbohydrate) *[1 mark]*.

### Pages 5-6 — Carbohydrates
**Q1** Complex carbohydrates *[1 mark]* (such as starch).

**Q2** E.g. obesity *[1 mark]*.

### Page 7 — Vitamins — Fat-Soluble
**Q1** Vitamin D helps the body to absorb other minerals (e.g. calcium) *[1 mark]*.

### Page 8 — Vitamins — Water-Soluble
**Q1** E.g. citrus fruit (e.g. oranges).
Scurvy is caused by a deficiency of vitamin C — citrus fruit, green veg and potatoes are rich in it, so will all do the job.

### Page 9 — Minerals and Trace Elements
**Q1** Fluoride hardens tooth enamel *[1 mark]* and helps prevent dental caries *[1 mark]*.

### Page 10 — Fibre and Water
**Q1** E.g. from sweating *[1 mark]* and passing urine *[1 mark]*.

### Page 11 — Healthy Eating Guidelines
**Q1** E.g. Peter meets the guidelines of the Eatwell Guide by eating lots of starchy carbohydrates (e.g. wholemeal toast, bread and rice) *[1 mark]*. He doesn't eat any fruit and vegetables — it is recommended to eat 5 portions of these a day *[1 mark]*. There are too many sugary and fatty foods, like jam, crisps and chocolate *[1 mark]*.
You could have also discussed his dairy intake — e.g. the cheese and yoghurt.

### Pages 12-13 — Nutritional Needs of Different Age Groups
**Q1 a)** Toddlers need calcium for healthy teeth and bone development *[1 mark]*.
**b)** Protein helps tissue growth and repair, which is important for teenagers who have rapid growth spurts *[1 mark]*.
**c)** Folic acid reduces the chance of birth defects in babies *[1 mark]*.
**d)** Elderly adults need vitamin B12 to help keep the brain healthy / prevent memory loss *[1 mark]*.

### Pages 14-15 — Diet-Related Health Problems
**Q1 a)** E.g. The likelihood of becoming obese can be reduced by doing regular exercise *[1 mark]* and eating less saturated fats and sugar *[1 mark]*.
You could also have mentioned making sure you don't consume more than the recommended daily calories.
**b)** Maintaining a healthy weight will reduce the risk of high blood pressure, which can cause CVD *[1 mark]*. Smoking damages the cardiovascular system — smoking less (or not at all) will reduce the risk of CVD *[1 mark]*.

### Page 16 — Energy Needs
**Q1** An obese person has a higher body weight than someone of healthy weight *[1 mark]* — this extra weight requires more energy and a higher BMR *[1 mark]*.

**Q2** $2000 \times 1.5 = 3000$ kcal *[1 mark]*.

### Pages 17-18 — Nutritional Analysis
**Q1** Fat: $30 \times 9 = 270$ kcal
Protein: $15 \times 4 = 60$ kcal
Carbohydrates: $30 \times 4 = 120$ kcal
Total: $270 + 60 + 120$ *[1 mark]*
$= 450$ kcal *[1 mark]*.

**Q2** E.g. You could use vegetable oils lower in saturated fats, e.g. rapeseed, to fry with *[1 mark]*, leave the skins on the potatoes to increase the fibre *[1 mark]*, and reduce the salt and sugar content by using herbs and spices instead of salt or sugary condiments *[1 mark]*.

### Pages 19-21 — Planning Meals for Different Groups
**Q1 a)** E.g. Use soya milk in the mashed potato rather than normal milk *[1 mark]*.
**b)** E.g. Swap the chicken for a replacement, e.g. Quorn™ or mushrooms *[1 mark]*.
**c)** E.g. Use a reduced-fat cheese *[1 mark]* instead of regular cheese.
You could have suggested an alternative to the bacon or removing the fat from it first.

# Answers

## Section Two —
## The Science of Food

### Page 23 — Why Food is Cooked

**Q1** Raw chicken can contain harmful bacteria *[1 mark]*. Cooking chicken at a high temperature destroys these bacteria and makes the chicken safe to eat *[1 mark]*.

### Page 24 — Heat Transfer

**Q1** Water is brought to the boil by conduction *[1 mark]* as particles in the pan vibrate and pass their heat energy on to the particles in the water *[1 mark]*, and by convection *[1 mark]* as convection currents in the water circulate warmer water around the pan until all the water in the pan is boiling *[1 mark]*.

### Pages 25-26 — Cooking Methods —
### Water-Based and
### Fat-Based

**Q1** E.g. You could braise the meat *[1 mark]*. This involves cooking the food slowly in a pot full of liquid and often herbs and vegetables *[1 mark]*. Braising is a gentle cooking method which helps to tenderise meat, making it a good method for tougher pieces of meat *[1 mark]*.

**Q2** Steaming is healthier than other water-based methods *[1 mark]* because there's no direct contact between the food and the water *[1 mark]*. This means steamed foods keep more of their nutrients / texture / colour / taste *[1 mark]*.

### Pages 27-28 — Cooking Methods —
### Dry Methods

**Q1** E.g. Both roasting and baking use dry heat to cook food *[1 mark]*, but roasting is usually done at a higher temperature than baking *[1 mark]*.

*You could also have said that fat is usually used with roasting but not baking, or that roasting browns food more than baking.*

**Q2** Grilling vegetables is healthier than roasting them because no fat is added *[1 mark]*.

### Page 29 — Changing Properties —
### Proteins

**Q1** The proteins in egg white denature when you fry an egg *[1 mark]*. The denatured protein molecules then join together and coagulate *[1 mark]*. Water becomes trapped between the protein molecules at this stage *[1 mark]*. This turns the egg white from a runny, clear liquid into a white solid *[1 mark]*.

### Page 30 — Changing Proteins —
### Carbohydrates

**Q1** E.g. Dextrinisation gives food a browner colour *[1 mark]* and a crispier texture *[1 mark]*.

*You could also say that dextrinisation gives food a different taste.*

**Q2** Starch granules absorb water when they're heated *[1 mark]*, causing them to swell *[1 mark]*. Between 62 °C and 80 °C, the granules burst and the starch is released into the water *[1 mark]*.

*You could also say that starch granules become softer when they are heated.*

### Pages 31-32 — Changing
### Properties —
### Fats and Oils

**Q1** Shortcrust pastry doesn't rise when it's baked because the gluten molecules in the dough have been 'shortened' *[1 mark]*. Fat rubbed into the flour *[1 mark]* gives particles a waterproof coating *[1 mark]*. This stops gluten forming long strands *[1 mark]*, so the dough cannot become stretchy or rise *[1 mark]*.

*You could have also mentioned the use of 'shortening' fat, which has no water and so there's no steam to raise the pastry.*

### Page 33 — Raising Agents

**Q1** Any two from: folding / beating / whisking / sieving / creaming / rubbing in *[2 marks]*.

**Q2** Bicarbonate of soda has an unpleasant alkaline taste *[1 mark]* that wouldn't be masked by the relatively plain taste of a sponge cake *[1 mark]*.

### Page 34 — Uses of Microorganisms

**Q1** Bacteria are added to pasteurised milk to produce yoghurt (an ingredient in tzatziki) *[1 mark]* — the bacteria ferment lactose (a sugar in the milk) to produce lactic acid, which thickens the milk and gives it a tangy taste *[1 mark]*.

## Section Three —
## Food Spoilage

### Page 36 — Food Spoilage

**Q1 a)** Whole milk *[1 mark]* — bacteria need moisture for growth. There is more moisture in whole milk than powdered milk *[1 mark]*.

**b)** A pizza at room temperature *[1 mark]* — bacteria grow more quickly in warmer conditions *[1 mark]*.

### Page 37 — Food Spoilage

**Q1** E.g. There is mould growing on the tomato *[1 mark]*.

*You can mention that the tomato smells off, that it looks different (cracked or wrinkly) or it tastes different / fermented.*

**Q2** Banana slices are exposed to the air, so enzymes will react with oxygen, causing browning *[1 mark]*. Lime juice is highly acidic *[1 mark]* — the change in pH will stop the activity of the enzymes and the banana slices won't brown *[1 mark]*.

### Page 38 — Storing Food Safely

**Q1** The food has not been stored correctly. The raw beef should be covered *[1 mark]* and stored on the bottom shelf of the fridge and the cake should be moved to a higher shelf *[1 mark]*.

**Q2** The cooked beef is a high risk food *[1 mark]*. Refrigerating it will slow the growth of bacteria and extend its shelf life *[1 mark]*.

# Answers

## Page 39 — Storing Food Safely

**Q1** Dried pasta should be kept in a cool, dry place (e.g. a cupboard) *[1 mark]* in its original packaging / a sealed container *[1 mark]*.

**Q2** Raw poultry will have a 'use by' date on the packaging *[1 mark]*. This is because bacteria can multiply quickly in the food and make it unsafe, so this date is given as a safety warning to the customer *[1 mark]*.

## Page 40 — Preparing Food Safely

**Q1 a)** Bacteria from raw meat or other high risk foods *[1 mark]* can contaminate other foods if they are prepared on the same chopping board that is not thoroughly washed *[1 mark]*.

**b)** Cats can carry bacteria in their fur / bodies *[1 mark]* and can contaminate food by eating it, walking over it or laying droppings on work surfaces *[1 mark]*.

*Pests include pet animals such as cats.*

## Page 41 — Food Poisoning

**Q1** E.g. The chef should cook the eggs to the correct temperature to destroy bacteria (above 75 °C) *[1 mark]*, use clean equipment to prevent cross-contamination *[1 mark]* and should follow personal hygiene procedures like washing hands etc. *[1 mark]*.

*Maybe you've put down that the chef could buy eggs from hens vaccinated against salmonella — that'd be good too.*

# Section Four — Where Food Comes From

## Page 43 — Grown Food

**Q1** E.g. Pesticides are used to stop crops being eaten / to control weeds / to control fungus growth *[1 mark]*. Chemical fertilisers are used to replace lost nutrients in the soil *[1 mark]*. However, pesticides and fertilisers can harm wildlife / wash into rivers, polluting them *[1 mark]*.

## Page 44 — Grown Food — GM Crops

**Q1** E.g. To make it pest-resistant *[1 mark]* (or to improve its growth / make it ripen quicker / add nutrients).

**Q2** E.g. Some people think that it isn't natural to alter the genes of crops *[1 mark]*. There may be negative health effects that we don't know about yet *[1 mark]*.

## Page 45 — Reared Food

**Q1** Free-range food is food produced from animals that are free to roam / live in natural conditions *[1 mark]*.

**Q2** Free-range animals require more land to rear than factory-farmed animals *[1 mark]*. They take longer to grow / use up more energy than factory-farmed animals *[1 mark]*.

## Page 46 — Caught Food

**Q1** A sustainable fishing technique does not damage the environment or catch more fish than can be replaced *[1 mark]*. Bottom trawlers may catch unwanted animals in their nets *[1 mark]* and destroy corals and the seabed *[1 mark]*.

## Page 47 — Waste Food and Packaging

**Q1** E.g. Simon should be careful not to overcook or burn the meal *[1 mark]*, should cook the correct portion sizes *[1 mark]* and should store any leftovers in the freezer *[1 mark]*.

**Q2** Cooked ham is a high risk food and can't be stored for long *[1 mark]*, so the offer encourages customers to buy more than they would be able to use or store *[1 mark]*.

## Page 48 — Waste Food and Packaging

**Q1** E.g. Manufacturing packaging uses up energy and non-renewable resources *[1 mark]*. Lots of packaging isn't recycled and ends up in landfill *[1 mark]*. Transporting foods with excess packaging uses more energy — this means more greenhouse gases are produced *[1 mark]*.

## Page 49 — Food Miles and Carbon Footprint

**Q1** E.g. 'Pick your own' strawberries might be fresher / tastier / more nutritious *[1 mark]* and cheaper *[1 mark]* than those from a supermarket. Strawberries picked at a local farm will be better for the environment as they'll have fewer food miles *[1 mark]*.

**Q2 a)** E.g. banana milkshake *[1 mark]*

**b)** E.g. Bananas have to be imported from tropical countries *[1 mark]*. Lots of energy is used to pasteurise and refrigerate milk *[1 mark]*.

*Obviously, there are many possible answers here — I just happened to be craving a banana milkshake at the time.*

## Page 50 — Global Food Production

**Q1** E.g. Higher sea levels could flood low-lying farmland *[1 mark]*.

## Page 51 — Global Food Production

**Q1** The UK has a suitable climate to grow a variety of crops / can afford to import foods *[1 mark]*. Sienna has a high income, so can afford to buy good quality food *[1 mark]*, so Sienna will have food security *[1 mark]*.

## Pages 52-54 — British and International Cuisines

**Q1** E.g. Glamorgan sausage — Wales — Cheese and leeks coated with breadcrumbs *[1 mark]*. Cornish pasty — England — Pastry containing beef, potato, swede and onions. *[1 mark]*, Haggis — Scotland — Lamb, suet, onion, oatmeal, spices and seasoning (traditionally encased in an animal's stomach) *[1 mark]*.

**Q2 a)** E.g. Japanese: Noodles, seafood (salmon, mackerel, squid), pickled vegetables, Wasabi paste *[2 marks]*

*Award 2 marks for 4 ingredients, otherwise 1 mark for 2 or 3 correct ingredients.*

# Answers

**b)** E.g. Japanese:
Sushi — Sticky rice, often topped or rolled with raw fish and seaweed *[1 mark]*.
Tempura — Seafoods, vegetables or meat coated with batter and deep-fried *[1 mark]*.
Ramen — Noodles in a soup, topped with vegetables, meat, eggs etc. *[1 mark]*.

### Pages 55-56 — Primary and Secondary Food Processing

**Q1** E.g. Walnuts are sorted into different sizes *[1 mark]* or crushed / pressed to make oil *[1 mark]*.

**Q2** Secondary processing uses primary processed foods *[1 mark]*. Wheat flour, which is a product of primary processing *[1 mark]*, is combined with other ingredients (yeast, water...) to make a dough which is cooked to make bread *[1 mark]*.

### Page 57 — Food Fortification and Modification

**Q1** Soya milk doesn't contain as much of some of the useful nutrients *[1 mark]* that are found in cow's milk. Soya milk is fortified (e.g. calcium is added) so the nutritional content is similar to cow's milk *[1 mark]*.

**Q2** Fortified foods already contain a great deal of added vitamins *[1 mark]*. Taking supplements as well could mean Gerardo is getting too much of certain vitamins, which could be dangerous *[1 mark]*.

### Page 58 — Food Fortification and Modification

**Q1** Colourings make the sweets more attractive and appealing for customers to eat *[1 mark]*.

**Q2** E.g. A consumer may have an additive allergy *[1 mark]* or believe an additive-free lasagne is a healthier option *[1 mark]*. They may be concerned about the long-term health effects of artificial additives *[1 mark]*.

## Section Five — Factors Affecting Food Choice

### Pages 60-61 — Influences on Food Choice

**Q1** E.g. People with low incomes will only be able to afford cheaper food options *[1 mark]*. This may lead to a poorer diet, as cheaper foods are often less healthy, e.g. highly processed, high in fat and sugar *[1 mark]*.

**Q2** E.g. A person working long shifts may have less free time to exercise *[1 mark]*. Sedentary lifestyles burn far less calories than active lifestyles *[1 mark]*. People who are stressed may eat more comfort food, which is often high in fat or sugar *[1 mark]*.

### Pages 62-63 — Cultural, Religious and Moral Food Choices

**Q1** E.g. People may buy Fairtrade products (with the FAIRTRADE Mark) *[1 mark]* as this means farmers are paid a fair wage for their products *[1 mark]*.

**Q2** E.g. They may not eat pork, or any products made from pigs *[1 mark]*. They can only eat meat that is halal (slaughtered in the Islamic way) *[1 mark]*.

### Pages 64-65 — Food Labelling

**Q1 a)** E.g. All ingredients must be listed to comply with EU law *[1 mark]*. People with certain dietary requirements can safely pick what to eat *[1 mark]*.

**b)** E.g. How to store the product, the product name, the weight or volume, cooking instructions *[2 marks]*.

There are other pieces of information you could have listed — see p.64. Award 2 marks for 4 correct pieces of information, otherwise 1 mark for 2 or 3 correct pieces of information.

**Q2** E.g. Traffic-light labelling to give guidance on the level of fat, salt and sugar *[1 mark]*, whether a product is suitable for a certain group such as coeliacs *[1 mark]*.

### Page 66 — Influences of Marketing

**Q1** E.g. The product may be re-released with reduced sugar or salt *[1 mark]* or added vitamins *[1 mark]*.

**Q2** Using film franchises helps manufacturers target certain age groups *[1 mark]* or persuade fans of a film to buy a product that they may not usually buy *[1 mark]*.

### Pages 67-68 — Sensory Testing

**Q1** E.g. Tasters should work on their own so they are not influenced by others *[1 mark]*, they should be allowed to drink water between samples to refresh the palate *[1 mark]*, and the tests should be carried out in similar rooms, with the same lighting, so that the food looks the same to each taster *[1 mark]*.

**Q2** E.g.

| Characteristic | Taster Ratings | | | | Average |
|---|---|---|---|---|---|
| | A | B | C | D | |
| Dryness | | | | | |
| Sweetness | | | | | |
| Saltiness | | | | | |
| Texture | | | | | |

Your table should have:
Room for four tasters *[1 mark]*
Two or more relevant characteristics *[1 mark]*
An 'average' column *[1 mark]*

# Glossary

| | |
|---|---|
| 5 a day | The Government recommends that everyone should eat at least five portions of different <u>fruits or vegetables</u> every day to promote good health. |
| additive | Something that's added to a food product to improve its properties. |
| aeration | When <u>air is added</u> to a mixture to help make it lighter, e.g. when making cakes. |
| allergy | An immune system response to a certain substance (an allergen), e.g. in fish, nuts and eggs. |
| alternative protein | A form of protein other than protein from meat which is suitable for vegetarians (e.g. tofu, TVP). |
| ambient food | A food that can be safely stored at room temperature. |
| amino acids | 'Building blocks' of the body that make up <u>proteins</u>. Our bodies can make non-essential amino acids, but we have to get essential amino acids from foods. |
| anaemia | A condition where you have a reduced number of red blood cells, e.g. from <u>iron deficiency</u>. |
| basal metabolic rate (BMR) | The <u>minimum</u> amount of <u>energy</u> needed to keep you alive each day. |
| basting | Putting the fat that has melted out of food back on top of the food while it's cooking. |
| 'best before' date | A date mark on the packaging of lower-risk food (e.g. dried pasta) that tells you when the food is expected to deteriorate in quality. |
| biological value | A measure of the amount of <u>essential</u> amino acids a protein-based food contains. |
| blanching | A cooking process that involves plunging a food, e.g. fruit or vegetables, into boiling water before cooling them in cold / iced water (often used before freezing). |
| blended sauce | A sauce made from liquid and a paste of cornflour and water / milk. |
| braising | Slow-cooking food in a covered pot that also contains liquid, herbs and vegetables. |
| calorie | A measure of the amount of <u>energy</u> in food. |
| caramelisation | The browning of sugar and the change in its flavour when it's heated above a certain temperature. |
| carbon footprint | A measure of the impact something has on the environment, based on the harmful <u>greenhouse gases</u> produced. |
| cardiovascular disease | Any disease related to the <u>heart</u> or <u>blood vessels</u>, e.g. <u>coronary heart disease</u> (caused by a build-up of <u>fatty deposits</u> in arteries) and <u>strokes</u>. |
| cholesterol | A <u>fatty substance</u> that is essential for cell membranes. Too much cholesterol in the body can increase the risk of <u>cardiovascular disease</u>. |
| climate change | A gradual change in climate patterns, e.g. due to <u>global warming</u>. |
| coagulation | When denatured proteins join together, changing the appearance and texture of food, e.g. when egg white turns solid. |
| coeliac disease | Where the digestive system is sensitive to <u>gluten</u> and can't digest it. |
| conduction | The transfer of heat energy through <u>solids</u> by the vibration of particles. |
| convection | The transfer of heat energy through <u>gases</u> or <u>liquids</u> by circulating currents. |
| cross-contamination | Transferring potentially harmful bacteria (or other microorganisms) from one thing to another, e.g. from raw food to ready-to-eat food via work surfaces, equipment or your hands. |
| cuisine | A style of cooking representative of a certain country or region. |

# Glossary

| | |
|---|---|
| danger zone | The range of temperatures (5 °C to 63 °C) in which bacteria multiply very quickly. |
| denaturation | When the chemical bonds holding proteins together break down, causing the protein to unravel. |
| dextrinisation | When starch molecules break down into dextrins after being exposed to dry heat. |
| diabetes | A disorder where blood glucose levels stay too high because the pancreas either can't produce enough insulin or the body resists it. |
| dietary reference values | Estimates of the amounts of nutrients people need in their diet. |
| dry frying | Cooking food in a pan without added fat or oil, sometimes called dry roasting. |
| Eatwell Guide | Government healthy eating guidelines in the form of a pie chart that shows how much or how little of each food group your diet should contain. |
| emulsifier | Something that's added to food to hold together ingredients that don't usually stay mixed, e.g. oil and water. |
| emulsion | A mixture of oily and watery liquids, e.g. mayonnaise. |
| enzymes | Biological catalysts that speed up chemical reactions. |
| factory-farmed | Produced by an intensive farming technique where reared animals have little room to move. |
| Fairtrade Foundation | A charity that partners with food suppliers to try and improve their working conditions and income. |
| fat-soluble vitamins | Vitamins (e.g. A and D) found in fatty foods, that the body can store in fat tissue for future use. |
| fertiliser | Organic matter or chemicals that make soil fertile by supplying it with nutrients. |
| flavour enhancers | Additives, e.g. monosodium glutamate (MSG), that boost the existing flavour of a food. |
| food miles | The distance a food product travels from where it's produced or grown to where it's sold. |
| food poverty | Where a person is unable to afford or access sufficient nutritious food. |
| food security | Having access at all times to enough safe, nutritious food for an active and healthy life. |
| fortification | When extra nutrients are added to a food, e.g. in breakfast cereals. |
| free-range | Produced by a farming technique where reared animals have more space to move and live naturally. |
| garnish | A small addition to a dish that adds extra colour or flavour, e.g. a slice of lemon. |
| gelatinisation | When starch particles swell and burst, thickening a liquid. |
| gelation | The process where foods, e.g. custard, are set by chilling or freezing. |
| gluten | A protein found in wheat flours, that makes doughs elastic (stretchy). |
| glycaemic index | A number used to indicate the effect a food has on blood sugar levels. |
| genetically modified (GM) food | Food that's had its genes altered to give it useful characteristics, e.g. GM tomatoes that have a longer shelf life than normal. |
| halal | Slaughtered or prepared using a method that follows Islamic dietary laws. |
| heat transference | When heat energy moves from one place to another — by convection, conduction or radiation. |
| high risk food | A ready-to-eat food that, if not stored correctly, could grow harmful microorganisms. |

# Glossary

| | |
|---|---|
| infused oil | An oil that has <u>absorbed</u> the <u>flavour</u> of herbs left to soak in it. |
| intensive farming | A farming method that produces <u>high yields</u> (production is often large-scale). |
| intolerance | An <u>inability</u> to eat a type of food without negative effects on the body. |
| julienne strips | Small, thin strips of vegetables. |
| jus | A thin sauce made from the juices from cooked meat. |
| kosher | Prepared food that follows the requirements of <u>Jewish dietary laws</u>. |
| lacto vegetarian | Someone who doesn't eat any meat, fish or eggs, but consumes milk and other dairy products. |
| lacto-ovo vegetarian | Someone who doesn't eat any meat or fish, but consumes milk, eggs and other animal products. |
| lactose intolerance | A digestive problem where the body <u>can't digest lactose</u> (milk sugars). |
| lecithin | A natural <u>emulsifier</u> found in egg yolks and soya beans. |
| macronutrient | A nutrient needed by our bodies in <u>large amounts</u>, e.g. fat, protein and carbohydrate. |
| marinate | To <u>soak</u> something in a mixture of things such as oil, wine, vinegar and herbs before cooking (to give it more flavour). |
| micronutrient | A nutrient needed by our bodies in relatively <u>small amounts</u>, e.g. vitamins and minerals. |
| microorganism | A tiny living thing that includes <u>bacteria</u>, <u>moulds</u> and <u>yeasts</u>. |
| mineral | A <u>chemical element</u> that our bodies need in small amounts. |
| mould | A microorganism that can spoil food such as bread, cheese and fruit. |
| nutritional analysis | Working out the nutritional content of a food or recipe. |
| obesity | A condition where the body has accumulated <u>too much fat</u>. |
| omega-3 and omega-6 | Groups of <u>essential fatty acids</u> that our bodies cannot make (they have to be eaten in our diet). |
| organic farming | A more natural method of farming, e.g. growing crops <u>without</u> artificial pesticides and fertilisers. |
| osteoporosis | A bone disease where bones weaken and become brittle. |
| pasteurisation | A process of heat treating food to destroy pathogenic bacteria. E.g. milk is pasteurised by heating it to around <u>72 °C for 15 seconds</u>. |
| pathogenic | Able to <u>produce disease</u>, e.g. some bacteria are pathogenic. |
| pesticide | A substance used to <u>kill pests</u> such as insects, weeds and fungi. |
| physical activity level (PAL) | A measure of how active you are / how much exercise you get. |
| plasticity | A property of fats that allows us to <u>spread</u> and manipulate them. |
| poaching | Cooking food in a pan of liquid below boiling point, e.g. poaching in a tasty sauce. |
| preservative | Something that's added to food to slow down the growth of bacteria and other microorganisms so that food lasts longer. |
| primary food processing | Changing <u>raw foods</u> to make them ready to eat or cook, or prepare them as ingredients for other food products. |

# Glossary

| | |
|---|---|
| protein complementation | Combining low biological value proteins to give enough of all the essential amino acids we need. |
| radiation | The transfer of energy through waves of radiation (there's no direct contact). |
| raising agent | Something that releases bubbles of gas that expand when heated. Raising agents are used to make cake and dough mixtures rise. |
| Ramadan | A month in the Muslim year in which most Muslims are expected to fast from sunrise to sunset. |
| ready meal | A pre-cooked meal that's frozen or chilled — you just need to heat it up. |
| reduction | A process that thickens and makes flavours of liquids more intense by evaporating water. |
| Reference Intake | Guidelines for the amount of energy and nutrients an average adult requires per day. Often shown as a percentage value on food labels. |
| rickets | A condition in children where bones are soft and weak. |
| roux | A sauce base made from plain flour and melted butter. |
| saturated fats | A group of fats that come mainly from animal sources and are solid or semi-solid at room temperatures. |
| seasonal foods | Foods that are only available at certain times of the year, e.g. British-grown asparagus is only available in May and June. |
| secondary food processing | Changing primary processed foods into other food products, e.g. flour into bread. |
| shelf life | The length of time a food can last without spoiling or losing its quality. |
| shortening | The effect of adding fat to a floury mixture, giving it a crumbly texture. Also the name of a fat with 100% fat content. |
| stabiliser | Something that's added to food to stop mixed ingredients from separating. |
| sustainable | A sustainable process or material is one that can be used without causing permanent damage to the environment or using up finite resources. |
| temperature control | Controlling the temperature of food during preparation, cooking and storage, to slow the growth of microorganisms or kill them off. |
| temperature probe | A device used to measure the internal temperature of a food and check it is cooked all the way through. |
| trace element | A mineral, but one that is needed by the body in even smaller amounts. |
| ultra heat treatment (UHT) | A heat treatment where milk is heated to around 135 °C for 1-4 seconds and packed into sterile containers. Also called ultra-high temperature processing. |
| unsaturated fats | A group of fats that come mainly from vegetable sources and are usually liquid at room temperature. |
| 'use by' date | A date mark on the packaging of food that is a safety warning about when the food is likely to be unsafe to eat, e.g. high risk foods. |
| vegan | Someone who doesn't eat any products derived from animals, e.g. meat, eggs and cheese. |
| vegetarian | Someone who chooses to not eat any meat. |
| vitamins | Organic compounds that are needed by the body in small quantities to keep us alive and healthy. |
| water-soluble vitamins | Vitamins that aren't stored in the body and should be taken in daily (B vitamins and vitamin C). |
| yeast | A microorganism that can spoil food (e.g. berries). Also, used as a raising agent in bread making. |

Glossary

# Index

# Index